Baja California
Land of Missions

Thank you Jim
for sharing the magic
that is Baja California!

Baja is a "time machine"!
David Klein
Dec. 23, 2018

The author at Mission San Ignacio in 2015.

Baja California
Land of Missions

A detailed history of the activities by the Spanish and others attempting to colonize the peninsula of California from 1535 to 1855

David Kier

David Kier

Dec. 23, 2018

M & E Books
El Cajon, California

M & E Books
PO Box 20121
El Cajon, California 92021

oldmissions@gmail.com
http://oldmissions.com
http://facebook.com/oldmissions

ISBN 978-1-4951-9121-3

Kier, David E.   1957-
Baja California Land of Missions

1. Baja California Missions; 2. Baja California Travel;
3. Spanish California History; 4. Mexican California History;
5. California History; 6. Baja California History;
7. Jesuits in Baja California; 8. Franciscans in Baja California;
9. Dominicans in Baja California;
10. Indians of Baja California

F1246. K57 2016   972'.202 KIE

Cover Images: Missions San Ignacio and Santa María over the
1757 Jesuit Map of California.
Cover design by Jay Lawrence.

Contents

Illustrations

Mission San Javier is just one of many amazing monuments to the energy and determination of the laborers, craftsmen and missionaries in the rugged interior of Baja California during the 1700s. Photo by Elizabeth Kier in 2009.

Preface

Many books have been written about the Baja California missions, the associated activities of the missionaries, and the Spanish government. Each of these books contains either a bit of information on all the missions or some detailed information about particular missions. One would need all the books ever written on Baja California missions to have anything approaching a complete picture of the activities that established and administered the missions in this harsh, desert peninsula that now is part of Mexico.

The objective of this book is to provide a single source of details about, and an accurate history of, the Baja California missions. Many of these details have often been hard to come by, and many were undiscovered or unpublished until the past century. Errors have frequently been passed from book to book. The present book attempts to correct errors in the written history; to do this, it uses whenever possible the original writings of the people who were at the missions.

For the Baja California traveler or Southwest history enthusiast, this book is designed to provide considerable data that would be helpful in enjoying a look back in time to the major events that took place at these missions. For the serious researcher who seeks even more details, the reference list at the end of this book will have great value. For many of the Baja California missions, all that is now known is included in this book. Inspiring the discovery and publication of more historic data would be another goal of this book, especially with the aim of updating future editions.

I have spent most of my life in pursuit of learning about events in Baja California. My first two travel guides were published in the early 1970s. In the years that followed, I wrote travel and historical articles for magazines about Baja California.

In 2012, I partnered with historian and author Max Kurillo to write the first book that correctly describes all forty-eight California missions in the order in which they were founded rather than based on which side of a line where they were located -- a line that did not exist when the missions were built.

San Diego de Alcalá was not the first California mission, it was just the first of twenty-one missions built north of a line drawn seventy-nine years after it was founded. Eighteen California missions were established *prior* to San Diego, on the peninsula to the south. Additionally, nine more missions were built in Baja California *after* San Diego was established.

Another fact Max Kurillo and I shared in *The Old Missions of Baja & Alta California, 1697–1834,* is that the California peninsula was the only California for at least 230 years before "Baja" was added to the name in 1769. A revised edition is planned for 2019, visit www.oldmissions.com.

Many volumes have been written about the Franciscan missions founded north of the peninsula in Alta California—since 1850, the U.S. State of California. The need for a thorough and modern report on the history of the missions founded in Baja California by the Jesuit, Franciscan, and Dominican Orders has long been clear. I am hopeful that I have fulfilled that need with this book.

Acknowledgements

My gratitude and appreciation go to so many people who have inspired me and assisted me in this project.

Thank you to the following: Max Kurillo for asking me to join him in writing our first book together and encouraging me to produce this one; Graham Mackintosh and Dr. Penny Pickett for proofreading and editing suggestions; mission photographer Jack Swords for being an outstanding resource of mission photos and he is recognized by INAH for his work; Jay Lawrence for designing the book's cover; Kevin Clough, Dr. Robert Jackson, Dr. Hans Bertsch, A.N. Muia, Christopher Glass, Tom Wimberly, and others who are credited with their photos, are appreciated dearly for their wonderful photography of many of the mission sites and churches; the many contributors on the Baja Nomad Internet forums, operated by Doug Means, who have shared their photographs or travel details; and thanks to the many authors who have written Baja California adventure and history books. Primarily inspiring me to write about Baja California were Choral Pepper and Howard Gulick. These two authors both had a deep passion for Baja California and promoted both history and adventure on the peninsula with their books and articles. I want to give special thanks to John Marnell for the suggestions and manuscript copy-editing he has provided to help this book have a first class appearance. John has spent many hours and days working with me on this book to keep me on-track to completion. Special thanks to my parents, Ed and Lynn Kier, who introduced me to Baja California and to camping and four-wheeling when I was only seven years old. That alone had a tremendous positive effect on my life. Finally, to my wife Elizabeth for her support and companionship as we traveled the many miles to see the beautiful, the ruined, and the vanished mission sites.

Baja California is a nearly 800-mile-long finger of rugged mountain and desert land. For a time, it was believed to be the mythical "Island of California." The peninsula is home to twenty-seven missions founded between 1697 and 1834 here numbered in the order of their founding. Nearly half of these missions were forced to relocate due to harsh conditions; some several times. The story of the mission system in Baja California continues to be one of historical fascination, as it has been for generations.

Introduction

The Spanish missions in Baja California have inspired many travelers to explore the California peninsula and research the vast connection they had with resilient people over the centuries. These old missions have sparked great passion in many to write about the colorful history of this first land to be called California. The missions are doorways to the past and themselves are the artifacts that we can continue to connect with.

Many of the mission churches are in their original condition and serve as parish churches today. Some are of more modern construction built on the original mission site. Others are unrestored, in ruins, or merely a bit of land which once was the location of a major undertaking that the mission system was. The mission enterprise in California was begun by Jesuit priests, continued by the Franciscan friars, and ended with the Dominican preachers. One historically significant fact of the missions in Baja California is that they include the first eighteen California Spanish missions. These eighteen were established over a period of seventy-two years, and before the so-called *first California mission* at San Diego was founded.

There was no national border when the missions were built. Politically, California was just a single Spanish province until 1804, by which time nearly all of the California missions had been established. To include the missions in Baja California with those in Alta California provides a more complete picture of the events as they actually occurred in history; that was accomplished with the 2012 book about the founding of all forty-eight California missions, *The Old Missions of Baja & Alta California, 1697-1834.*

Details about the twenty-seven Baja California missions are provided in this book, and will serve to complement the vast amount of information previously published about the twenty-one Alta California missions. The 800-mile-long peninsula of Baja California is the home of the oldest California missions, the newest California mission, and twenty-seven missions in total. Nearly half were moved at one time or another and have multiple locations. The last California mission to remain in operation also was in Baja California. The Missions of Baja California, of *Old California,* are an important part of the history of the Southwest, California, and Mexico.

Mission buildings often began as stick shacks followed by adobe structures. These were later replaced by larger stone churches at some locations. This sketch by Charles Larson is an impression of Mission Santa María's appearance circa 1770.

California Discovered

California was first believed to be an island with the name coming from the popular novel *Las sergas de Esplandián* with its romantic description of a land ruled by women who were "armed with gold, as they knew of no other metal." Such visions must have had the effect of attracting explorers. *California* became the name for the land from Cabo San Lucas north. There was no *Baja* (Lower) California until there was an *Alta* (Upper) California, and that was not until the Spanish occupied Alta California, following the expedition of 1769. The terms *Antigua* (Old) and *Nueva* (New) were also used to describe the peninsula and the "new" land to the north.

The first landing of Spanish sailors on the shores of California was made in late 1533 or in 1534. The exact date is unknown since the landing was made by a crew who were on the run after a mutiny. They were led by Fortún de Jiménez and are believed to have landed at or near La Paz. Jiménez and twenty others were killed by the natives. The survivors re-crossed the Gulf of California to report on the event and on the abundance of black pearls they had seen.

On or about May 5, 1535, the conqueror of Mexico himself, Hernán Cortés, came to California and attempted to build a colony at La Paz, he named the place Santa Cruz. It lasted less than two years because the land and its people were too harsh, and most of the colonists Cortés brought over had perished.

On July 8, 1539, Cortés sent Francisco de Ulloa with three ships to explore the west coast of Mexico. Ulloa went north to the head of the gulf, then came south along the eastern shore of California, proving it was not an island as had been envisioned. Ulloa rounded Cabo San Lucas and sailed north again over halfway up the peninsula before returning to

Acapulco. The California as an island idea would not die so easily, and maps continued to show California surrounded by the sea. More expeditions would try to prove or disprove that theory.

In 1540, Hernando de Alarcón sailed north to the Colorado River Delta while Melchior Díaz led a land expedition north, and is believed to have gone into California, making Díaz the first European to come to California by crossing the desert instead of the sea. Both men were part of the Francisco Vázquez de Coronado expedition to explore the north. Díaz died from a bizarre injury shortly after crossing the Colorado River into California. Where Melchior Díaz was buried has been a mystery for close to 500 years (see page 227 for the Díaz story link). Documents and maps from the voyages of Ulloa and Alarcón named the new land California.

In 1542, Juan Rodríguez Cabrillo sailed up the west coast of California and landed several times, naming points and bays northbound, and eventually came into San Diego Bay (calling it San Miguel). Cabrillo continued to sail north and reached the Channel Islands, where he died from a leg injury.

In 1596, Sebastián Vizcaíno established a colony at Cabo San Lucas that lasted only two months. In 1602, Vizcaíno led an expedition of 200 men on three ships up the California coast. Vizcaíno would give his own chosen names to many locations that Cabrillo had previously discovered and named. That is how San Miguel became San Diego, for example. At least sixteen more voyages across the gulf were made by 1668 to exploit the peninsula for its potential wealth, and most failed. Priests sometimes traveled to California on these expeditionary ships with hopes of converting the native population to Christianity. In September, 1668, Padre Juan Cavallero Carranco documented the time spent with Captain Francisco de Lucenilla. The final lines of Padre Cavallero's report illustrate the difficulties and disappointments of this and perhaps previous California expeditions:

"All of the California Indians are poor and naked, and there is no need to seek riches from them for each gives what he has. I conclude by stating again that no private individual should attempt to carry out this conquest; and particularly they should not be poor, since then all will be ruined and fail as has happened on more than twenty voyages which have been made. However, if Our King and Lord (may God guard him) counsels all those who go, they will do the greatest service to God imaginable by removing a great number of souls from the devil's power. With this I end the true report of the unhappy voyage to the Californias."

Fifteen years would pass until the next expedition to California.

Alarcón's ship in 1540 as it struggles at the confluence of the Colorado River and Gulf of California, drawn by F.S. Dellenbaugh. Longboats from his ship traveled some distance up the Colorado River.

Why Spanish Missions are in Baja California

The Spanish government used the Catholic Church to help it colonize the New World; the church was ambitious to convert native people to Christianity. That process was deemed the best method to instruct the local population how to live and work like Europeans and speak Spanish. The native Indians of California were generally referred to by the missionaries and Spaniards as *gentiles, pagans, heathens* or *savages* before they joined the mission and as *neophytes* after joining. The word "reduced" is also used by missionary writers to indicate those natives who have been assimilated (baptized) into the Catholic faith.

When the Spanish soldiers and Catholic priests arrived in the Indian homeland, they were usually met with either curiosity or hostility. Sometimes one was followed by the other, but eventually the mission would be established. Using food to entice them, missionaries could get the Indians to provide labor to help build the mission and to help with agriculture and livestock.

A mission was not simply a church, but an entire enterprise that would be the center of a community. Irrigation canals (*acequias*) and reservoirs (*pilas*) for the crops were a vital part of the mission. Missions were named for saints or holy sites that often shared the name of a financial sponsor's family member. The Indian name for the location was often attached which helped distinguish one mission from others with the same saint's name.

Missions were founded throughout the Western Hemisphere for some 200 years before advancing to California. The missionaries trained at and received supplies from the missions in Mexico which made the California mission program possible.

Missions had the objective to convert the Indians from hunter/gatherers to becoming farmers tending crops and livestock. As new colonists would arrive in California, they would live among fellow Spanish citizens and not be in fear of attack as had occurred to some of the first European arrivals. Another goal of the missions was to develop ports along the Pacific Coast to resupply the Manila Galleon enroute from Asia to Acapulco between the years 1565 and 1815.

Mission churches and altars were designed to dazzle the converts. Most of the native Californians had never seen walls with a roof above and had never heard the sound of large ringing bells. Paintings of the saints and benefactors were framed in gold leaf. Once the huge stone churches were built, especially in these remote locations, the curiosity and awe-inspiring size was amazing to the primitive population as much as it is to travelers today.

Usually, a mission center (*cabecera*) had some satellite chapels with farms. These were known as *visitas* (mission visiting stations). The mission priest would visit them periodically and conduct services. Visitas were typically located at existing Indian settlements (*rancherías*) that also had a good supply of water. Some visitas were very productive and had large stone chapels. Some would become missions, but a few mission sites would later be reduced in importance to being only a visita. Rancherías sometimes were relocated as the Indian tribes were often nomadic within a defined territory, following food sources. Some of the visita ruins were impressive and mistaken for being missions by more modern travelers. The best known visitas of Baja California include San Juan Londó, Magdalena, La Presentación, San Miguel (de Comondú), San Pablo, San Juan de Dios, and San Telmo. Ruins at Londó and San Pablo remain

7

impressive to see into the twenty-first century. Most others have collapsed into rubble, been washed away by floods, or plowed over by farmers.

Missions in California were founded by three Catholic Orders: The Jesuits (1683-1767), the Franciscans (1769-1823), and the Dominicans, also known as "The Order of Preachers" (1774-1834). While all three orders belong to the same church, each order has unique solemn vows, teachings, and practices. Unlike the other orders that replaced them in California, the Jesuits did not restrict or imprison the Indians who joined their missions.

The Jesuits, often referred to as the Black Robes for their manner of dress, immersed themselves into the native Indian languages so as to be better able to teach and gain their needed cooperation. What the Jesuits did that wasn't always popular was insist the Indians destroy their idols and religion and give up polygamy. The Pericú Revolt of 1734 was inflamed by these imposed rules.

Establishing a Jesuit mission had specific requirements. Once a suitable site was found, permission was obtained, financing was found, and a priest had to be made available. The lack of Jesuit priests often delayed opening a new mission for long periods. When the Jesuits were removed and replaced with the Franciscans, this arrangement ended and mission operations would be placed under civil authority and control.

All sixteen of the Jesuits in California were removed from their missions and taken from the peninsula in February 1768. The Franciscan Order, chosen to replace the Jesuits, arrived to take on their duties in April 1768. Within a year, the Spanish government gave Junípero Serra (Franciscan president of the California missions) the task of occupying Nueva California, the land to the north of the peninsula.

Spain was concerned that Russia or England would soon advance on it. The name of the peninsula was now modified to either Antigua (Old) California or Baja (Lower) California.

The Franciscans and later the Dominicans, under civil authority, were tasked with the continued conversion of California for Spain. The Indians began to be treated more as tools to achieve that goal. They were forced to stay at the missions once they joined the church and the men were beaten for a variety of reasons. The native Californians never achieved the equality of citizenship during the mission years.

The missionaries established and operated twenty-five missions on the peninsula of California for Spain. Two more missions were established by a Dominican priest during the Mexican period that followed. Those two are not universally accepted as true missions by all historians. In Alta California, nineteen missions were founded for Spain. Two more were founded during the Mexican period as well.

Missionaries often found it necessary to relocate their missions, usually to a better source of water for irrigation. Almost half the missions moved some distance and a few moved as much as ten to fifty miles (see also page 183).

A mission's name was sometimes changed or altered with the move and sometimes not. This caused confusion about Baja California missions for some, in past years.

Today, we use the word "mission" to apply to the church building itself or ruins of the former church buildings. However, when missions were operating, it was a more encompassing enterprise than just a church. Missions resembled a small colony, with agriculture, irrigation, hospital, and often a military presence.

The Missions and Missionaries

Jesuits

Padre Eusebio Francisco Kino, Padre Jean Baptiste Copart, and Padre Matías Goñi with soldiers commanded by Admiral Isidro de Atondo y Antillón sailed to La Paz, arriving on April 1, 1683, to begin a colony. Their new mission was named Guadalupe, but it failed to enlist many of the hostile coastal Indians. When supplies also failed to arrive, they abandoned the seaside colony on July 14, 1683. As they sailed away, the Spanish soldiers needlessly fired their cannon on the natives dooming any hopes of bringing the California Indians into their trust. See map on page 60.

Once the Spanish regrouped on the mainland, they made another crossing. With the second attempt, a new mission colony at San Bruno, fifteen miles north of Loreto, was begun on October 6, 1683. The Indians were friendlier at San Bruno and that eliminated one problem for the Spaniards. Kino and Atondo were able to explore the land to the west in December 1684. They were the first Europeans to reach the Pacific Coast of California by land. San Bruno survived longer than Guadalupe at La Paz but was abandoned on May 8, 1685. Reasons included the lack of good water, outbreaks of scurvy, and not having enough provisions needed to survive. Remains of the hilltop Spanish fort at San Bruno are the oldest European ruins of any kind in Lower or Upper California.

Ruins of the 1683 Spanish fort at San Bruno. Photo by Ed Vernon.

Padre Kino came to realize that for missions to be successful in California they would need to be supported for a time by the missions across the gulf in Mexico. Kino also concluded that any success in California would necessitate that Spanish soldiers be placed under Jesuit control. A dozen years would pass before the Jesuits could try again.

Spain agreed to the Jesuit proposal for autonomy over the California missions and soldiers, but the Jesuits would have to obtain their own financing for the operation. A *Pious Fund* was established to secure endowments from wealthy Europeans for the California missions. See Appendix E on page 211.

Once permission to return to California was granted by the Mexican Viceroy on February 5, 1697, Padre Juan María de Salvatierra worked closely with Kino on the project. Sadly, for Kino, he would be prevented from joining Salvatierra because of some Indian uprisings on the mainland that his superiors believed only he could resolve. Padre Francisco María Píccolo would follow Salvatierra to California in place of Kino.

A permanent California occupation for Spain began with the founding of the mission at Loreto in 1697. The Jesuit Order would establish seventeen missions, numerous mission satellite chapels and farms, and a network of well-built roads, all on what had been thought by many to be an island. Once California was confirmed as being attached to the continent by the 1746 Padre Fernando Consag sea expedition, efforts got under way to establish missions to the north.

For over seventy years the Jesuit Order of priests operated the missions. The Jesuits purpose in California was to learn the Indian languages, convert the natives to Christianity, teach them European methods of living, and to occupy the land for the King of Spain. They needed to have authority over the soldiers to prevent brutality against the Indians. After many years of missionary work, rumors claimed the Jesuits were disrespecting the King's authority, and amassing great wealth. These rumors spread about the Jesuits later proved to be false. The Jesuits were removed from California practically as prisoners in February of 1768.

Franciscans

In April 1768, the Franciscans led by Padre (now Saint) Junípero Serra arrived to continue the California mission program but under Spanish civil control. The Franciscans were soon given new instructions to expand far north, along the Pacific Coast, and occupy the ports of San Diego and Monterey. This northern territory had no name, so it was simply called New (Nueva) California or Upper (Alta) California. The peninsula began to be referred to as Old (Antigua) California or Lower (Baja) California, after the 1769 Gaspar de Portolá/Junípero Serra expedition to San Diego and Monterey. After just five years, the Franciscans handed over Baja California mission duties to the Dominican Order of Preaching Friars, in May 1773.

Dominicans

The Dominicans operated the missions of Baja California for eighty-two years through a period of growth, dramatic changes, and disappointments. To some historians, their methods were harsh and unbending to the needs of the native Indians they hoped to Christianize and convert to modern living. What is clear is that the Dominicans constructed many missions, including the cut stone churches at San Ignacio, Santa Gertrudis, and San Borja.

The Dominicans inherited a land that was already in decline yet they performed vaccinations to try to save the lives of those infected by European diseases. They endured years of neglect during two wars (1810-1821 and 1846-1848) and a change of government in Mexico that attempted to secularize their missions. Still, they remained on the peninsula the longest of the three orders assigned to mission duties in California.

The following is a summary of some of the events pertaining to the Dominicans in California, called Baja California after 1769:

July 24, 1768: A request for the administration of some of the Jesuit-founded missions of Baja California was made by Dominican Fray Juan Pedro de Iriarte y Laurnaga. Iriarte was Procurator General for the Province of Santiago de Mexico, residing at the Royal Court of Madrid. He asked especially for those missions between the 25th and 28th degrees of north latitude.

December 17, 1769: King Carlos III decided that ten Dominican fathers, destined for the nearest former Jesuit missions, should go there but left the exact posts unspecified.

January 17, 1770: The Procurator General, Fray Juan de Dios de Cordoba, recommended that Iriarte's petition be granted, that the requested territory of Baja California be allocated, since there was urgent need for the conquest of Nueva California as a check against foreign encroachment.

June 15, 1770: Juan Pedro de Iriarte and Juan de Dios de Cordova asked the King for a grant of twenty-four missionaries, at royal expense, for the missions of Baja California.

July 10, 1770: Iriarte issued a circular to the convents of the three Spanish Provinces of the Dominican order, announcing that the king had granted them a mission field in Baja California and calling for volunteers.

April 30, 1772: The division of California was settled and the Dominicans accepted all Baja California while the Franciscans had Alta California, as far north "as they can extend their spiritual conquests." This arrangement was approved by the Council of the Indies on May 11, 1775.

September 1772: Two boats were used to bring the Dominicans to California from San Blas. Storms separated the boats and disaster fell on one. The storm, disease, and bad food forced one boat back to shore at Mazatlán. On board the doomed boat was their leader, Padre Iriarte. After arriving at Mazatlán, he was taken to San Sebastián, where he died.

October 14, 1772: The successful boat with nine Dominican priests and one lay brother arrived at Loreto. Ten days later one of those priests died. Nearly six months passed before news arrived that the other boat carrying Dominicans had wrecked and their leader, Padre Iriarte, and two other priests had died.

May 12, 1773: The eighteen Dominicans who survived the September shipwreck arrived at Loreto in two different boats that were far more seaworthy. Three days later the padres were given their mission assignments. See Appendix D on page 205. Now with twenty-six Dominicans in California, each of the missions was assigned two, except for the far north missions of Santa María and San Fernando, which shared two priests. The Indian neophytes of Mission Santa María were transferred to Mission San Fernando in 1775.

September 21, 1773: Padre Luis Sáles arrived in Loreto after being delayed by his illness from the disastrous events of a year earlier. Sáles was assigned to Mission Guadalupe.

March 26, 1804, was the date when Alta and Baja California became two separate political districts. Politically it had been just one California before, with forty-four Spanish missions founded. In 1810, Mexico declared its independence from Spain. The final four missions in the Californias are considered "Mexican missions" and were not built with Spain's influence or involvement.

Mission Names

This book will primarily utilize the common or popular modern name used rather than the full, official name. In the next section are the common names followed by the original, official name. Mission Santa Rosalía de Mulegé is the full name for the mission commonly known simply as Mulegé. Every mission name, spelling, and pronunciation is in Spanish. For example, Mulegé is pronounced "Moo-leh-HAY." Mission San Luis Gonzaga Chiryaqui was commonly called San Luis during the Spanish period, but in modern times it is known as San Luis Gonzaga. Chiryaqui was the native Indian name for the location.

Official mission names usually stayed with the mission if it moved to a new location. However, after the move, a mission might be called by the new location name, creating confusion as to how many missions existed. La Paz/ Todos Santos; Dolores/ La Pasión; Calamajué/ Santa María; and San Miguel/ El Descanso are examples of one mission known by another name following a relocation.

El Camino Real (The Royal Road), also called "The King's Highway" was the line of communication and supply between the missions. Photo by Harry Crosby in 1967. The trail was often little more than a route across the desert with larger rocks moved to either side. Where they were needed, switchbacks were carved into the mountainsides to permit mules to transport cargo and personnel to cross the rugged land.

Baja California Missions
(Founding Year, Common Name, *Official Name*)

1 - 1697 LORETO
   Nuestra Señora de Loreto Conchó
2 - 1699 SAN JAVIER
   San Francisco Javier Biaundó
3 - 1705 LIGÜÍ
   San Juan Bautista de Ligüí (Malibat)
4 - 1705 MULEGÉ
   Santa Rosalía de Mulegé
5 - 1708 COMONDÚ
   San José de Comondú
6 - 1720 LA PURÍSIMA
   La Purísima Concepción de Cadegomó
7 - 1720 LA PAZ/ TODOS SANTOS
   Nuestra Señora del Pilar de la Paz
8 - 1720 GUADALUPE
   Nuestra Señora de Guadalupe de Huasinapí
9 - 1721 LOS DOLORES
   Nuestra Señora de los Dolores
10 - 1724 SANTIAGO
   Santiago el Apóstol Aiñiní
11 - 1728 SAN IGNACIO
   San Ignacio de Kadakaamán
12 - 1730 SAN JOSÉ DEL CABO
   San José del Cabo Añuítí
13 - 1733 SANTA ROSA
   Santa Rosa de las Palmas
14 - 1737 SAN LUIS GONZAGA
   San Luis Gonzaga Chiryaqui
15 - 1752 SANTA GERTRUDIS
   Santa Gertrudis*

16 - 1762 SAN BORJA
San Francisco de Borja Adac
17 - 1766 CALAMAJUÉ/ SANTA MARÍA
Nuestra Señora de Columna/ Santa María de los Ángeles

The above listed missions were founded by the Jesuits.

* Some contemporary books have either *Santa Gertrudis la Magna* or *Santa Gertrudis de Cadacamán* as the full official name. Jesuit texts indicate such names are inconclusive.

18 - 1769 SAN FERNANDO
San Fernando de Velicatá

After the Franciscans founded San Fernando, they continued to establish missions from San Diego on north.

The following missions were founded in Baja California by the Dominican Order while the Franciscans were establishing missions in Alta California:

19 - 1774 EL ROSARIO
Nuestra Señora del Rosario de Viñadaco
20 - 1775 SANTO DOMINGO
Santo Domingo
21 - 1780 SAN VICENTE
San Vicente Ferrer
22 - 1787 SAN MIGUEL
San Miguel Arcángel
23 - 1791 SANTO TOMÁS
Santo Tomás de Aquino
24 - 1794 SAN PEDRO MÁRTIR
San Pedro Mártir de Verona

25 - 1797 SANTA CATALINA
  Santa Catalina Virgen y Mártir
26 - 1810* DESCANSO
  El Descanso (San Miguel la Nueva) **
27 - 1834 GUADALUPE
  *Nuestra Señora de Guadalupe***

* Year location was developed. New mission built in 1830.
** Not a mission authorized by the Spanish government

The 2012 book, *The Old Missions of Baja & Alta California, 1697-1834,* covered the founding of all forty-eight California missions in accurate chronological order.

Baja California history enthusiasts Marian and Neal Johns along El Camino Real, some thirty years after the Harry Crosby photograph on page 16 at the same spot.

Spanish Missions of Baja California

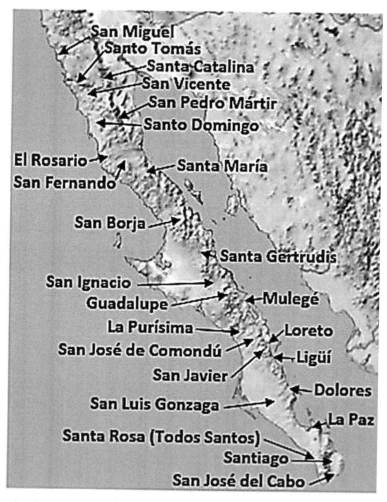

The final two missions of El Descanso and Guadalupe del Norte were founded during the Mexican Period and are located just north of and just east of Mission San Miguel, respectively.

Padre Juan de Ugarte was one of the most energetic of the Jesuit missionaries. Serving the California missions from 1700 for thirty years until his death. Ugarte was responsible for building the first ship in California, *El Triunfo de la Cruz* launched on September 14, 1720. The ship was used to establish the mission at La Paz in 1720. On May 15, 1721, it sailed from Loreto to the north end of the Gulf of California to again prove the land of their missions was not an island.

El Camino Real in Baja California

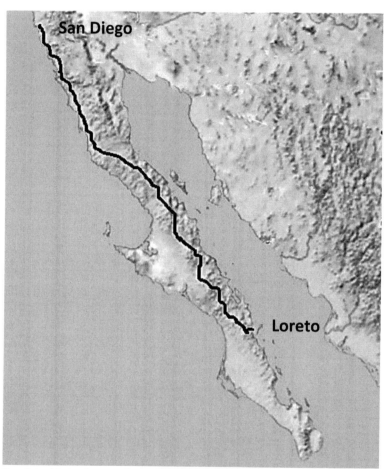

Depicted is just one of several routes of El Camino Real. Additional routes connected all the missions, north and south of Loreto. An exciting new website with a map giving the accurate location of El Camino Real, from Loreto to El Rosario, has been produced by backpack hikers and historical researchers Kevin Branscum and Geneviève Mattar: http://caminorealbaja.com/

El Camino Real

The Royal Road, or "King's Highway" as it is popularly known, connected all the California missions and was expanded to include branches to Indian settlements (*rancherías*), satellite chapels (*visitas*), and supply beachheads. Originally, El Camino Real was a pathway for tax revenue to get to the king from all his territories. Many Camino Reals are in the New World. In the Californias, El Camino Real was a communication and supply line rather than a route for tax revenue. The following is part of a report by Jesuit Padre Miguel Venegas. This historical account was completed on November 7, 1739. The name "Camino Real" has been edited into **bold** font in the following quote for emphasis of how long the mission road system had been called by that name:

"It is this impossibility which the missionaries have surmounted by dint of their personal labor, the aid of the Indians already converted and civilized and the assistance of the soldiers. In order that the work might be fairly distributed among all the Indians, in proportion to the advantage which they would derive from the building of these roads, the fathers adhered to the following plan in making this distribution. First of all, they had a main highway **camino real** built through the center of the mission district extending through its entire area and running lengthwise from south to north. All the *rancherías* [Indian settlements] belonging to the mission worked together in building this road, for it was of common advantage to them all. Then each ranchería assumed the responsibility for building a special road leading from its settlement and joining the **camino real** which was, so to speak, the main trunk-line in which all the separate roads from the rancherías terminated. By this means connection was finally made with the headquarters of the mission.

"When these roads were being built it was necessary for the father missionaries to be present and to direct the work. And they had to spend many days in moving about, circling hills and climbing peaks, in order from the summits to spy out the stopping places which were least inaccessible. Moreover, many tools were needed for distribution among the Indians: pickaxes, crowbars, hoes, sledge hammers, shovels, ordinary hammers, levers, ropes, and other tools of this sort. There was least work to be done in the stony areas on the hills and slopes. Yet even here the labors were very great. For the road had to be made wide enough for the passage of animals and pack-trains. The work crews spent many days in removing the loose stones from which they formed low walls or borders along both sides. Nor did they stop until they struck bedrock; thus in some places they dug to the depth of a *vara* [33 inches] and in others went even deeper, so that some of the roads were shaped like ditches or the canyons of streams.

"Then came the harder work—the smoothing, insofar as that was possible, with sledge hammers, pickaxes, and crowbars of the outcroppings and jutting points of solid rock which barred the passage of travelers. When their tools did not avail they had recourse to fire in order to split the rocks and break them up; then they used levers and ropes in order to remove them and set them rolling into the *barrancas* [ravines] and over the precipices. But the work was most painful and the difficulty greatest when they had to pass over the hills and mountains. This happened very often, since there would be no other place where they could build the road. Here they had to follow routes on steep slopes which fell away into barrancas. In such places they had to contend with the solidity of the mountains and the hardness of the rocks while they labored to break off outcroppings and sharp points and to clear away the stones great and small which lay in the way. In many narrow passes between the hills, where the powers of man were insufficient to break a trail, they were obliged to set thick stakes along the sides and to fill the intervening space with branches and the trunks of trees, putting earth on top, forming bridges, as it were, which would make it possible to pass from one side to the other in these ravines."

During the Jesuit period (1697-1768), the road was built to high standards and with a great degree of engineering. Much of it can still be seen, 250 to 300 years after it was constructed across the desert and mountains of Baja California. Indeed, many miles are still in use today by ranchers and tourists on mule back.

The Franciscans and Dominicans did not have the same skill or interest in road building as the Jesuits. With only a few exceptions, the Camino Real north of Mission San Borja resembles not much more than a cattle trail -- if any trail exists at all. The Jesuits were removed from California before serious road construction to Mission Santa María could be initiated. The route is generally known, thanks to letters from mission-era and post-mission-era travelers. Modern roads have been built over the mission trail in many places. Thanks to many history researchers, we know the route as it travels through Baja California.

One major El Camino Real researcher of the twentieth century was *Lower California Guidebook* author Howard Gulick, who documented and mapped the mission road from Loreto to El Rosario, in 1954. Another, and maybe better known was Harry Crosby, who began traveling the trail in 1967 as a photographer for a book about the founding of the Alta California missions. Crosby then went on to research his own 1974 book, *The King's Highway in Baja California*.

In 1977, Harry Crosby commissioned a series of detailed maps of the Camino Real from Loreto to San Diego. They were published in the Winter 1977 edition of *The Journal of San Diego History* and can be seen online at www.vivabaja.com at this link: Harry Crosby's Photos and El Camino Real Details.

El Camino Real also went south from both the Loreto and San Javier missions to connect the many missions in that direction. Ligüí/Malibat, San Luis Gonzaga, Los Dolores, Pilar de la Paz, Santiago, Santa Rosa, and San José del Cabo were all connected by El Camino Real.

The old mission road from Loreto to San Diego is often mentioned in books, but the route from San Diego to San Francisco was made famous with decorative bells created by Mrs. A. S. C. Forbes starting in 1906. Those bells began a tradition that has marked the route to the present time. The old mission trail north of San Diego is now mostly modern paved highways and streets bearing the name "El Camino Real."

Next, we will examine each of the twenty-seven missions in Baja California in the order in which they were founded from 1697 to 1834.

The First Four California Missions

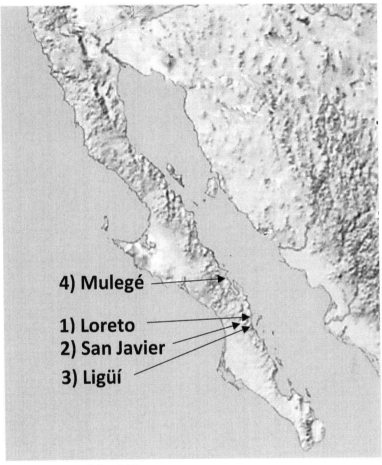

4) Mulegé

1) Loreto
2) San Javier

3) Ligüí

1) Loreto Conchó, 1697
2) San Francisco Javier, 1699
3) San Juan Bautista de Ligüí, 1705
4) Santa Rosalía de Mulegé, 1705

Mission of Loreto. Photo by Jack Swords.

#1 Nuestra Señora de Loreto Conchó (1697-1829)

On October 19, 1697, Padre Juan María de Salvatierra with the financial contribution of Juan Caballero, founded the mission of Loreto at the native Indian ranchería of Conchó. The mission began as a simple structure inside the *presidio* (fort) until the natives accepted the Spanish on their land. The mission did not begin without incident. On November 13, 1697, the natives had decided not to only accept the gifts of food that followed the religious instruction but also to attack the mission and take it all. Arrows and rocks struck the compound and attack came from all sides, Salvatierra wrote. The Spanish soldiers were successful in defending their presidio and saving the mission. The chief came forward and offered peace with the Spaniards shortly after sunset.

In 1699 construction on a larger, adobe church was started outside the presidio and this was completed on September 8, 1704. New missions would be built out from Loreto on a road network that would become known as *El Camino Real*, securing the land for the King of Spain. Forty-eight missions would eventually be established in both Lower and Upper California over the next 137 years.

In 1740, Padre Jaime Bravo began construction on a larger church built of stone and mortar whose walls survive to this day. The importance of Loreto as the capital of California would continue into the next century. The Jesuits would not be so enduring.

Two important visitas of Loreto were San Juan Londó and San Ignacio (not the same location as the future mission named San Ignacio). Londó was thought by some to be a mission because of its chapel's size and elaborate stone construction.

All sixteen California Jesuits were ordered expelled from the peninsula in 1767 by a Royal Decree which was personally read to the assembled Jesuits on December 26 by newly appointed Governor Gaspar de Portolá. The Jesuits boarded a ship at Loreto on February 3, 1768, and two days later began the long journey back to Europe, joining along the way with their Jesuit brothers who were also expelled from other parts of the New World.

On Good Friday, April 1, 1768, the Franciscan friars, led by Junípero Serra, landed at Loreto and began the operation of the missions. In a year, Serra would lead an expedition north into unexplored lands to establish missions at San Diego and Monterey. The Franciscans became very involved in the new territory from San Diego north. They agreed to share California mission duties with the Dominican Order of Preachers. A boundary line was marked dividing the Franciscan and Dominican jurisdictions on August 20, 1773, by Padre Francisco Palóu at Médano Valley about twenty-six miles south of today's international border.

In May 1773, the Dominicans replaced the Franciscans at all peninsula (Baja) California missions. In addition, they were given the unconverted land to establish new missions of their own and fill the void along El Camino Real between San Fernando de Velicatá and San Diego.

The line between Franciscan and Dominican zones was moved north in 1788 about ten miles to Arroyo del Rosarito by Padre Luis Sáles and remained the dividing point between Baja California and Alta California until the end of the war with the United States in 1848, when it was moved north one final time, about sixteen miles.

On March 26, 1804, California was officially divided into two political regions of Baja California and Alta California each with a governor. Forty-three of the forty-eight missions had been founded in California before that date. By the end of the mission period the Jesuits had founded the first seventeen missions, the Franciscans founded twenty-two, and the Dominicans founded nine. In all, twenty-seven missions were in Baja California and twenty-one in Alta California.

The Loreto mission was so damaged by floods from a hurricane in 1829 that it was closed and the capital of Baja California was eventually relocated to La Paz. The bell tower was later destroyed in the earthquake of 1877. A modern bell tower was added at Loreto in 1955, however it does not match the style or scale of the original.

The Loreto mission and museum are a highlight of any visit to Loreto, and its importance is inscribed over the doorway, which reads: Cabeza y Madre de Las Misiones de Baja y Alta California (Head and Mother of the Missions of Lower and Upper California).

Photo by the author in 2017.

The lists of missionaries provided for each mission may include visiting missionaries in addition to those assigned to a mission. Records are incomplete so missionaries may have been active additional years outside the ones shown. Gaps in the list indicate the data was lost or missing and give mission history researchers additional purpose. It is this author's hope that more names and years can be added to future editions of this book.

Missionaries recorded at Loreto:
Jesuit
Juan Salvatierra 1697-1704 and 1707-1717
Francisco Píccolo 1697-1699 and 1718-1729
Juan de Ugarte 1701
Jerónimo Minutili 1702-1703
Pedro de Ugarte 1704
Jaime Bravo 1705-1720 and 1728-1744
Julián Mayorga 1707
Clemente Guillén 1718 and 1748
Juan Mugazábal 1720-1761
Gaspar Trujillo 1744-1748
Juan Armésto 1747-1752
Johann Bischoff 1753-1757
Francisco López 1755-1762
Lucas Ventura 1757-1768
Julián Salazar 1758 and 1763-1765
Ignacio Tirsch 1762-1763
Juan Villavieja 1765-1768
Francisco Franco 1767-1768

Franciscan
Junípero Serra and Fernando Parron April 5, 1768
Juan Ramos de Lora 1769-1772
José Murguía 1770
Vicente Santa María 1771-1772
Fernando Parron 1772

Dominican
Vicente Mora (to 1800) and Martín Zavaleta May 15, 1773
Nicolás Muñóz 1779
Francisco Galistéo 1779-1789
Miguel Hidalgo 1781
José Armésto 1790
Antonio Berraguerro 1793
José Herrera 1793-1794
Caietano Pallás 1794-1798
Pedro de Acebedo 1795
Miguel Gallégo 1795 and 1810
Pablo María de Zárate 1796
Plácido Sanz 1798, 1804
Vicente Belda 1798-1802
Rafaél Arviña 1802-1804
Antonio Lázaro 1806
Ramón López 1812-1816

Mission San Javier. Photo by the author in 2009.

#2 San Francisco Javier de Biaundo (1699-1817)

Having heard of an Indian settlement named "La Vigge" hidden away amid a circle of virtually impassable mountains, Padre Francisco María Píccolo forged his way from Loreto up through rocky arroyos and precipitous passes until he reached the site. The trek was arduous indeed. Thinking the settlement's name was La Vigge, which to the Indians meant "mountain," each time he came upon a new group of Indians and inquired of the way to La Vigge, they would send him off to a new series of mountain peaks. At an Indian settlement named Biaundo, he founded Mission San Francisco Javier de Biaundo on May 11, 1699 with financial support from Juan Caballero. This was at today's Rancho Viejo and about five miles north of the final mission site, developed later by Padre Juan de Ugarte.

During a drought that occurred around the year 1710, the original mission headquarters was obliged to move to the nearby visiting station and farm of San Pablo, a location that turned out to be so promising that after Padre Juan de Ugarte came to replace Padre Píccolo, he moved the mission there. Costing over a million pesos, possibly gained from profits of pearl fisheries supposedly discouraged by the Jesuits, the ambitious new mission was endowed with a belfry, spires, and altars that required many years of construction. The church was built from 1744 to 1758 and remains as the finest preserved original mission in California. Cut in stone above the lintels of the door is the date 1751. Today it is the most architecturally impressive mission on the peninsula, remaining in good condition, and continues to serve the need for religious functions.

Spectacular black lava cliffs rise hundreds of feet behind it, casting the mission's white Moorish domes and bell tower into stark relief. To the north, east, and west, great double doorways open into the mission. Within its vaulted interior, light filters through the peninsula's first stained glass windows, falling on three gold-leaf altars shipped from Mexico and reassembled.

Dominating the main altar is a statue of Saint Francis Xavier, surrounded by eight revered oil paintings of saints and the Holy Trinity. A spiral staircase reaches the choir loft. Presently three bells are in the tower, two dated 1761 and a third 1803. It is interesting that an early Jesuit description of this mission endowed it with eight bells, more than any other mission. Visitas of San Javier include Santa Rosalía (later named Santa Rosalillita), San Miguel (now San Miguel Comondú), and La Presentación. Visita San Miguel was very productive and some Jesuits served there in preparation for their future mission work.

Mission San Francisco Javier reached a high degree of prosperity. The stone mission was constructed under the leadership of Padre Miguel del Barco, who was at San Javier for thirty years beginning in 1738. Of all the peninsula missions, this one is perhaps the most rewarding to visit.

The twenty-two-mile automobile road from Loreto was opened at the end of 1952 and for sixty years was a tough ride usually done in a truck or Jeep. A paved highway now connects Loreto with San Javier, but it is subject to washouts after summer storms.

Missionaries recorded at San Javier:
Jesuit
Francisco Píccolo 1699-1703
Juan de Ugarte 1702 and 1704-1730
Juan Basaldúa 1703-1704
(Mission moved in 1710)
Juan Mugazábal 1718-1719
Agustín Luyando 1730-1738
Miguel Barco 1737-1768

Franciscan
Francisco Palóu April 5, 1768
Fernando Parron 1768
Juan Escudero 1769-1771
Ramón Uson 1771-1772
Vicente Santa María 1772-1773

Dominican
Manuel Pérez (to 1794) and Domingo Ginés May 15, 1773
Gerónimo Soldevilla 1784-1810
Mariano Yóldi 1791-1792
Miguel Gallégo 1794
Romantino de la Cruz 1812

The Ligüí monument in 2012, about 300 feet from original mission site. A visit in 2017 revealed that this monument had vanished. The site had been washed away by flash floods. Photo by the author.

Ligüí mission foundation ruins in 1975. Flash floods had destroyed the site by 2001. Photo by Robert Jackson.

#3 San Juan Bautista de Ligüí/Malibat (1705-1721)

Mission San Juan Bautista de Ligüí was founded by the Jesuit Padre Pedro de Ugarte in late November of 1705 among the Monqui Indians. Padre Ugarte left Loreto on November 21 with a band of soldiers and previously converted Indians. Pedro Ugarte located his new mission near the beach, twenty-one miles south of Loreto. Ligüí was the Monquí name for the location. Eventually, the mission was repopulated with Cochimí Indians, who had called the location Malibat. A third group of Indians lived on the nearby islands. They were the fierce Pericú tribe who resisted conversion and often raided the mission. The mission name often was known simply as San Juan in Jesuit letters. Today, a small village near the mission site is named using the original, Ligüí.

Padre Pedro de Ugarte's first church was made from sticks, but he was eventually able to get help from the *neophytes* (baptized Indians) to make an adobe chapel. Two boys would become Ugarte's assistants, but when he fashioned clothes for them to cover their nakedness, the other members of the tribe laughed and teased them so much that they removed their garments when they went outdoors.

The mission was never very successful because of the poor water supply and Indian raids. A Jesuit was not always stationed here after ill health forced Ugarte to depart for the mainland in 1709. Another blow to the mission happened when its benefactor, Juan Bautista López, went bankrupt and the mission's funding was lost although the Jesuits found the means to continue it. Ugarte was replaced by Padre Francisco Peralta, who served San Juan Bautista de Malibat mission from 1709 to 1711. The last Jesuit assigned to the mission was Padre Clemente Guillén from 1714 to 1717 and again from 1719 until the mission was closed in August 1721.

With a new benefactor providing funds, Padre Guillén reestablished the mission over fifty miles south at a better site called Apaté. The new mission was named Los Dolores and was much more successful than the mission at Ligüí/Malibat had ever been.

The Ligüí mission site was obliterated by flash floods after the arroyo widened and began to undermine the site between 1973 and 2001. Construction of Mexico's Highway One has been named as the cause for the arroyo's diversion into the mission church foundations. A large white cross serving as a monument to the mission was erected next to the original site. Unfortunately, it was washed away as the arroyo continued to widen. Nothing marked the spot in 2017.

The village of Ligüí is on Highway One about twenty-one miles south of Loreto, just before the highway climbs into the Sierra la Giganta mountains. Turn off the highway at the town's sign and head straight for the gulf coast. Another sign is reached in a half mile that shows a left turn for Playa Ligüí beach. The right fork goes south to the village of Ensenada Blanca. Just past the fork, now in the arroyo, was the location of the mission. Just beyond the original site, next to the beach road, was a white cross and outlined area serving as a monument for the vanished mission. This was 0.6 mile from Highway One and it too was swallowed by the widening arroyo.

Jesuit Missionaries recorded at San Juan Bautista de Ligüí:
Pedro de Ugarte 1705-1709
Francisco Peralta 1709-1711
Clemente Guillén 1714-1721

The Loreto visita of San Juan Londó in 2009 with Elizabeth Kier.

La Magdalena visita reservoir (*pila*) ruins north of Mulegé. Photo by the author in 2015.

Mission Santa Rosalía de Mulegé. Photo by the author in 2017.

Mission Santa Rosalía de Mulegé. Photo by the author in 2017.

#4 Santa Rosalía de Mulegé (1705-1828)

Starting out November 21, 1705 and traveling nearly 100 miles north from Loreto, Padre Manuel de Basaldúa founded the mission of Santa Rosalía at the Cochimí settlement of Mulegé. The mission's benefactor was Nicolás de Arteaga and his wife Josefa de Vallejo.

Santa Rosalía de Mulegé mission is located on a rare Baja California river, about two miles from the gulf coast. The river proved to be a problem as the mission and its farmlands were nearly destroyed by flash floods in 1717 and again in 1770.

The stone church constructed in 1766 overlooks the river from a high ledge, and is safe from floods. This building project occurred less than two years before the Jesuits were expelled from the New World. Spain's King Carlos III had been convinced that the Jesuits were amassing treasures and not paying the Crown its due. Inventoried when the missions were ceded to the Franciscans, the missions true poverty was confirmed, as there were no treasures discovered.

The Franciscans replaced the Jesuits in California in 1768. Padre Francisco Palóu wrote that he considered having this mission moved following a flood in 1770 that destroyed the fields below the mission. A proposed new location was a place called Magdalena.

La Magdalena (or "Santa María Magdalena" in some maps and books, following an error made by Arthur North in his 1910 *Camp and Camino in Lower California*) is just fifteen miles north of Mulegé. Stone building ruins, an aqueduct, and a reservoir could be seen until recently, but no record of who built it or when it was built is known. Flash floods in 2014 erased most of the Magdalena ruins. An old church ruin is about five miles further to the west, close to the village of

San José de Magdalena. It is sometimes referred to as a Dominican mission visita site, but it is more likely to be post-mission period construction.

Even though mission activities ceased in 1828, the church at Mulegé continued to serve the newly arrived Mexican people who replaced the vanishing Indian population. Activities at the mission church continued to be documented through much of the middle to late 1800s. Priests assigned to Mulegé often were placed in charge of the other mission churches of the region (Loreto, Comondú, San Ignacio), as was noted in the *Libro de Gobierno* (Government Book) of 1873.

The mission is just west of the highway bridge over the Mulegé River. A signed, paved access road to the mission is just south of the bridge.

Missionaries recorded at Mulegé:
Jesuit
Juan Basaldúa 1705-1709
Francisco Píccolo 1709-1718
Nicolás Tamaral 1717
Sebastián Sistiaga 1718-1733
Francisco Osorio 1725
Juan Luyando 1727-1733
Everard Hellen 1731-1732
William Gordon 1733-1734
Pedro Nascimbén 1735-1754
Benno Ducrue 1755
Joaquín Trujillo 1756-1757
Francisco Escalante 1757-1759 and 1760-1768
Julián Salazar 1759-1760

Franciscan
Juan Ignacio Gaston April 5, 1768
Francisco Gómez 1768-1769
Benito Sierra 1769-1773
Pedro Arriguibar 1771

Dominican
Joaquín Valero (to 1800) and Antonio Luésma May 15, 1773
José Naranjo 1783
José Herrera 1783-1794
Miguel Gallégo 1795-1798
Rafaél Arviña 1796-1797
Domingo Timón 1798-1800
Vicente Belda 1802-1805
José Portela 1812
Tomás de Ahumada 1815-1821

California Indians with a killed deer, by Padre Ignacio Tirsch, 1762-1768.

1906 interior view of the Comondú mission church that was demolished thirty years later. Photo by Arthur North.

San José de Comondú chapel. Photo by the author in 2017.

#5 San José de Comondú (1708-1827)

The fifth California mission was founded by the Jesuit Padre Julián de Mayorga about thirty miles northwest of Loreto, on a stream that flowed west to the Pacific Ocean. The new mission name was a combination of the Indian name for the site (Comondú) and the Spanish name, "San José de la Giganta," given to it by Padre Juan María de Salvatierra, Loreto's founder. The Marqués de Villapuente, José de la Peña Castejón y Salcines was the mission's benefactor.

The first enclosed church building here was small and made of adobe blocks. It replaced a simple thatch-roofed shade structure made from local trees. Padre Mayorga hoped to construct a larger church, but a smallpox epidemic delayed its construction. Stone masons were not available, so the larger church was also made of adobe. It was built on a stone foundation and completed in October 1716. The footing can still be seen today. The new church and attached storeroom walls were nearly seventy feet long by twenty-one feet wide and ten feet high. The walls were three feet thick, so the interior width was only fifteen feet.

In 1717, two mission visiting stations or visitas were transferred to the jurisdiction of Comondú from Loreto. They were San Juan Londó and San Ignacio (not the 1728 Mission San Ignacio site). The visita of San Ignacio was twenty-two difficult miles south of San José de Comondú. Because the visita of San Ignacio was such a productive source of food, Padre Mayorga took frequent trips there to help develop it further. Two more miles south was another visita, but developed for Mission San Javier and named San Miguel. Together, the visitas of San Miguel and San Ignacio provided more food than many of the other peninsula missions could.

The Jesuits assigned Padre Guillermo Gordon from 1734 to 1737 to the San Miguel visita to relieve both Padre Mayorga of Comondú and Padre Agustín Luyando of San Javier. Some have called San Miguel a separate mission because of this, but Jesuit records show it was never a mission. The location is now known as San Miguel Comondú.

Padre Julián de Mayorga had been ill for some time and twenty-eight years after he founded San José de Comondú he passed from this life on November 10, 1736. The Jesuits must have been anticipating that day, because they decided to move Mayorga's mission to the visita of San Ignacio, just a couple of weeks later. Some say the mission first moved to nearby San Miguel for a year while San Ignacio was being prepared. The mission name remained unchanged with the move, and the name San Ignacio was eliminated once it became the new mission site. The loss of their padre and then the sudden move from their homeland caused great strife among the Comondú neophytes. The original mission location was renamed Comondú Viejo and is today located between the ranches of San Juan and La Presa.

A massive cut-stone church complex was constructed at the new location during the years 1754 to 1760. Even as epidemics were killing off the population the church was built to attract and serve. What had been the largest mission church in California fell into ruin and was demolished in 1936. A side chapel to the main mission church was preserved and is what stands today in the town of San José Comondú. San José Comondú can be reached by paved road from the south or by rough roads from the east and north.

Missionaries recorded at San José de Comondú:
Jesuit
Julián Mayorga 1708-1736
(Mission moved in 1736)
Franz Wagner 1737-1744
José Rondero 1745-1751
Gaspar Trujillo 1748
Franz Inama 1751-1768

Franciscan
Antonio Martínez April 5, 1768
Vicente Imas 1771
Tomás de la Peña 1771-1772
Juan Prestamero 1771-1773

Dominican
Cristóbal de Vera and Andrés Souto May 15, 1773
José Estévez 1790-1791
Pedro de Acebedo 1790-1793
José Aivár 1792
Ricardo Texéyro 1794-1796
Jorge Coéllo 1797-1798
Plácido Sanz 1803-1810
José Antonio Sánchez 1812
Tomás Mansilla 1825-1826

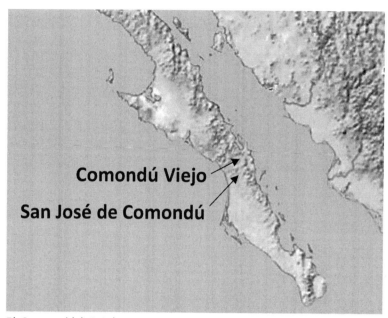

5) Comondú (Viejo) 1708-1736 and Comondú 1736-1827

Walled-up entrance to 1760 mission church in 1906. Photo at San José de Comondú by Arthur North.

Ruins at the 1708-1736 mission site, Comondú Viejo. Photo by the author in 2017. This was the home of Padre Julián Mayorga.

The same mission site ruins in 2001. Photo by Jack Swords.

La Purísima mission church in 1906. Photo by Arthur North is facing north. The graveyard is on the east side and has a large tomb.

La Purísima mission ruins in 1956. Photo by Howard Gulick, facing east. The only remains of the mission complex in 2017 were two tombs. One of them is seen in the 1906 photo.

#6 La Purísima Concepción de Cadegomó (1720-1826)

The sixth California mission was founded on January 1, 1720, by Jesuit Padre Nicolás Tamaral at a site originally discovered in 1712 by Padre Francisco Píccolo while exploring southwest from Mulegé. Píccolo found an ideal site with many rancherías nearby and promised the natives to provide them with their own padre and a mission. With an endowment from the Marqués de Villapuente, and access trails constructed, Padre Tamaral arrived to begin the new mission. The first structure was made of branches and straw. From 1720 to 1722, he split his time between the new mission and the San Javier mission visita of San Miguel, where he had been assigned since 1717. In early September 1722, Tamaral ended his duties at San Miguel and began a full-time commitment to La Purísima.

The mission prospered for several years. By 1730, the Cochimí Indian neophyte population had grown to 1,996 members. Padre Tamaral had great success growing grapes, pomegranates, figs, sugarcane, guava, sapote, lemon, wheat, and corn. No doubt the abundant food was a great attraction to the area's Indian rancherías. Some have written that around the year 1735, the mission was moved ten miles south. While there are some foundation stones at a place called Purísima Vieja, Jesuit documents are lacking.

A Jesuit report made in 1744 indicates the mission was productive, owed nothing, and had a population of 156 families. A Franciscan report made in 1772 describes the church as made of stone and some adobe, roofed with *tules* (reeds or bulrush, *Schoenoplectus acutus*). It had vineyards and many fig trees and pomegranates. Cotton was grown to clothe the Indians. A plague of locusts had destroyed the wheat and corn crops in 1771. A Dominican report in 1793 describes an adobe church seventy feet by eighteen feet, poorly furnished. The priest's house was a spacious adobe room with a library containing 200 books.

Epidemics crushed this mission's prosperity as they had at many others on the peninsula and the native population of La Purísima dropped to sixty-one by 1800. That was just five years after the neophytes from the abandoned mountain mission of Guadalupe had been transferred to La Purísima.

La Purísima functioned as a mission for 106 years before it too was abandoned for lack of native Indians. Mexicans from the mainland arrived later to take up farming in the lush valley. The irrigation canals built by the missionaries and their neophytes are still functioning close to 300 years later.

Photography shows that the mission church was still being used in the early 1900s, but fell into ruin in the years that followed. By 1950 only small portions of the church walls remained. In 2017, only two crypts and some rubble are all that mark the mission's location in the town of La Purísima. The site is reached by paved road from the south or a graded dirt road from the east.

Missionaries recorded at La Purísima:
Jesuit
Nicolás Tamaral 1720-1730
Francisco Osorio 1725-1726
Sigismundo Taraval 1730-1732
Jacobo Druet 1733-1753
Benno Ducrue 1753-1754
Franz Inama 1755-1757
Johann Bischoff 1758-1766
Juan Díez 1766-1768

Franciscan
Juan Crespi April 5, 1768
Miguél de la Campa y Cos 1768-1769
Juan Ignacio Gaston 1768-1773
Antonio Martínez 1769 (from Comondú)
Francisco Eschasco 1771
Martín Palacios 1771

Dominican
Francisco Galistéo and Juan Antonio Formoso May 15, 1773
José Estévez 1775-1782
Martín Zavaleta 1783
José Antonio Sánchez 1793-1822
Domingo Luna 1822-1826

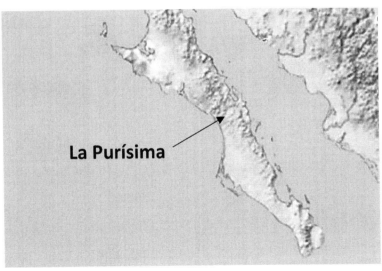

La Purísima

6) La Purísima, 1720

La Paz mission first location plaque, in La Paz. Photo by Jack Swords. Second mission location photo, see page 88.

Third and final location of Mission Pilar de la Paz, in Todos Santos. Photo by Joseph R. Slevin in 1919.

#7 Nuestra Señora del Pilar de la Paz (1720-1748 at Airapí, 1748-1840 at Todos Santos)

The seventh California mission was founded by two Jesuit padres: Jaime Bravo and Juan de Ugarte. The site was near the shore of La Paz Bay and locally known as Airapí. The journey to La Paz Bay began at Loreto on the Jesuit ship *El Triunfo de la Cruz* built in Mulegé from lumber cut in the mountains to the west. Padres Bravo and Ugarte were joined by Padre Clemente Guillén from Mission San Juan Bautista at Malibat (Ligüí), who came by land with soldiers and neophytes.

La Paz was unique as no one single Indian group lived there; instead it was visited by several peninsula tribes of Guaycuras and Pericús (who came from the islands off shore). These various groups often were at war with each other. Padre Jaime Bravo would remain at La Paz until 1728 but always with four to twelve soldiers for protection due to perceived hostilities. Padre William Gordon replaced Bravo for the next five years.

One visita of Mission Pilar de la Paz was named Ángel de la Guarda. It was established in 1721 by Padre Bravo about twenty miles south, at a mountain-top oasis. On the western foot of the same mountain is a church ruin named El Novillo. El Novillo was sometimes shown on maps as a mission, but it was not. In 1725, Padre Bravo established another visita of La Paz about fifty miles to the south and close to the Pacific Coast. Bravo never recorded an Indian name for the location, but he named it Todos Santos. This visita was so productive that it became a separate mission in 1733 with the name Santa Rosa de las Palmas bestowed upon it.

In October 1734, after months of unrest, the various tribes in the cape region rebelled. They murdered Padre Nicolás Tamaral at San José del Cabo and Mission Santiago's Padre Lorenzo Carranco was also killed, along with his two servants. At La Paz, a soldier who was guarding that mission was killed. Padre Sigismundo Taraval of the Santa Rosa mission was saved by his soldiers, who dragged him away just before the natives began to attack.

Following the rebellion, there were two years of vacancy at La Paz. Between 1737 and 1748, Jesuits from both the Santa Rosa and San Luis Gonzaga missions visited La Paz and conducted mission tasks. In 1748, the bay-side mission of La Paz relocated to Todos Santos, replacing the younger Santa Rosa mission already there. The mission name remained officially Nuestra Señora del Pilar de la Paz, but it was nearly always called Todos Santos after the move. See also the chapter on Mission Santa Rosa beginning on page 89.

When the Franciscans replaced the Jesuits in 1768, the population of neophytes was reported to be about ninety. An adobe church measuring sixty-seven feet by twenty-five feet was built in 1786 by the Dominicans. The native population had doubled to 181 by 1800. The mission remained at the same location until 1825 when it was moved a mile south, where the church is today, in the town plaza.

No remains of the original Pilar de la Paz mission at La Paz Bay are known to exist; however, a plaque on a La Paz city side street marks a possible location. The modern church in La Paz is sometimes called the mission site, but it is three blocks north and one block east from the plaque. Some local historians believe the mission was even a little further south, where old sketches showed palms growing.

The 1733-1825 Todos Santos site, that was home to two missions, is now a playground by a modern church from 1970. The 1825 mission site is the downtown church, where newer construction was added to older walls and foundations. Mission functions ceased about 1840, but church services continued on for the newer population arriving from the mainland of Mexico.

Missionaries recorded at Pilar de la Paz:
Jesuit
Jaime Bravo 1720-1728
William Gordon 1728-1733
(Vacant 1734-1736)
Bernhard Zumziel 1737-1750
(Mission moved to Todos Santos in 1748)
Johann Bischoff 1751-1752 and 1767-1768
Karl Neumayer 1752-1764
Francisco Franco 1764-1766

Franciscan
Juan Ramos de Lora April 5, 1768
José Murguía 1769
Marcelino Senra 1771
Miguel Sánchez 1771-1773

Dominican
José Fernández Salcedo and José Armésto May 15, 1773
Mariano Fernández 1790-1811
Jacinto Tiól 1812-1820
José Duro 1822
Gabriel Gonzáles 1825-1840 and 1850-1855

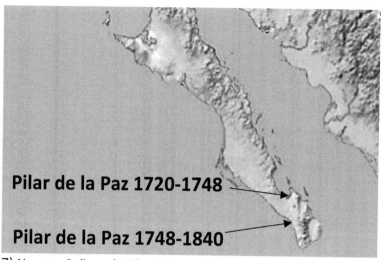

Pilar de la Paz 1720-1748

Pilar de la Paz 1748-1840

7) Nuestra Señora de Pilar de la Paz Airapí (at Bahía de la Paz) and Nuestra Señora de Pilar de la Paz (at Todos Santos)

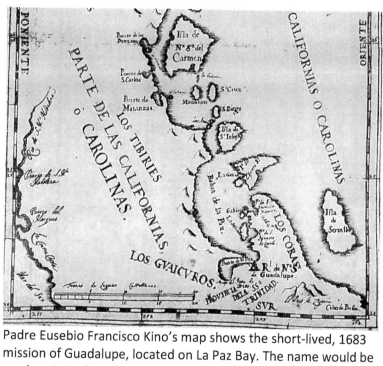

Padre Eusebio Francisco Kino's map shows the short-lived, 1683 mission of Guadalupe, located on La Paz Bay. The name would be used again in thirty-seven years at a very different location.

Guadalupe

The Guadalupe mission ruins are uphill from this arroyo crossing.

Guadalupe mission ruins in 1996. Photo by Max Kurillo.

Guadalupe mission ruins in 1999. Facing southwest from what was once inside the church. Photo by Edward Vernon.

Guadalupe mission ruins in 2017. Facing northwest from inside the church. Photo by the author.

#8 Nuestra Señora de Guadalupe de Huasinapí (1720-1795)

The history of the eighth California mission began in 1719 when Padre Juan de Ugarte discovered a forest of güérivo trees (*Populus brandegeei*) from which he could construct California's first ship, *El Triunfo de la Cruz*. According to the missionaries, the Cochimí Indians of the region (who helped cut and transport the lumber) requested a mission of their own.

On December 26, 1720, Jesuit Padres Juan de Ugarte and Everardo Hellen arrived at the Indian settlement of Huasinapí and began to establish the mountain mission. Padre Hellen served at Guadalupe for fifteen years, except when he was ill and removed to rest at Mulegé in 1724, and once again in 1726. Over 2,000 natives were baptized by the Jesuits here in those first fifteen years at Mission Guadalupe.

Just two years after its founding, the people of Guadalupe mission suffered the destruction of crops and native fruits (pitahayas, berries, etc.) by swarms of locusts. The food stores of wheat and corn at the mission helped save them from starvation. The Cochimí neophytes also gathered up dead grasshoppers, then dried and cooked them to supplement their diet. Sadly, dysentery broke out from that action and many lost their lives.

The mission church floor was tiled, and a 1744 report by Padre Juan Antonio Balthasar said that Guadalupe had "the finest church in California." Tragedy followed heavy rains in November 1744 when a mission wall collapsed and killed 100 neophytes. A new stone and adobe mission church was built around 1750 and it is those foundation stones that can be seen today.

Unfortunately, the diseases introduced by the Europeans decimated the native California population and the Guadalupe mission was abandoned in 1795. The surviving seventy-four neophytes were transferred to La Purísima.

In 1834, another mission named Guadalupe was founded in the far north area of Baja California. To avoid confusion, that northern mission is typically called "Guadalupe del Norte." The 1720 mission in the south became known as "Guadalupe del Sur" or known locally as "Ex-misión de Guadalupe."

Guadalupe de Huasinapí is accessed by a dirt road from Mulegé. Take it twenty-five miles west and then twenty more miles north. Another road to Guadalupe from San José de Magdalena was washed out and made impassable in 2014. A local guide may be required to locate the ruins.

Missionaries recorded at Guadalupe:
Jesuit
Everarado Hellen 1720-1735
Ignacio Nápoli 1724
Francisco Osorio 1726
Joseph Gasteiger 1735-1754
Benno Ducrue 1755-1768

Franciscan
Juan Sancho de la Torre April 5, 1768
Andrés Villaumbrales 1770
Manuel Lago 1771-1772

Dominican
José Santolárria and Nicolás Muñóz May 15, 1773
Luis Sáles 1773-1778
Joaquín Valero 1783
Rafaél Arviña 1792-1795

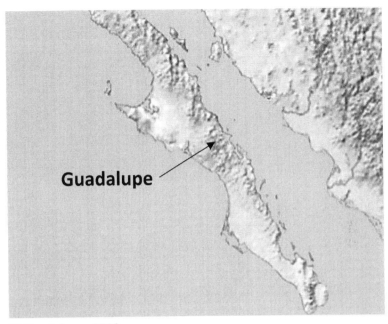

8) Guadalupe, 1720

Fascinating cave paintings are found in many locations in central Baja California. They have been dated back 500 to over 1,000 years in the past. Photo by Choral Pepper.

Authors Erle Stanley Gardner and Choral Pepper inspired many to seek history and adventure in Baja California with their writing.

Choral Pepper and the author in 2002. Choral Pepper was a great inspiration for him to write this book. More about her is at http://vivabaja.com/choralpepper/

Los Dolores

Los Dolores Apaté mission ruins in 1998. Photo by Kevin Clough.

Los Dolores Apaté ruins in 2014. Photo by Ashek. In 2017, these walls were seen by the author and still standing.

Los Dolores Chillá (La Pasión) ruins in 2017. Photo by the author.

Los Dolores Chillá (La Pasión) ruins in 1950. Photo by Marquis McDonald.

#9 Nuestra Señora de los Dolores (1721-1741 at Apaté and 1741-1768 at La Pasión de Chillá)

The mission of Los Dolores began because of the need for a mission between Loreto and La Paz following the failure of the mission at Ligüí/Malibat. The new mission was also known as "Dolores del Sur" to distinguish it from an important early visita of the Loreto mission that was named Dolores.

In 1720, Padre Clemente Guillén investigated the site of Apaté along the gulf coast during his overland trip from Malibat (Ligüí) to help start the La Paz mission. Guillén found fresh water near the beach at Apaté by digging a shallow well. Guillén also found running water in a canyon about two miles west of the beach.

On August 2, 1721, with new funds guaranteed by the Marqués de Villapuente, Guillén founded the mission of Nuestra Señora de los Dolores de Apaté. The mission may have been established quite close to the beach initially, but within two years was moved into the canyon. A stone-walled church, dam, aqueduct, reservoir, and other mission structures were built there, and ruins of them remain to this day.

In 1734, Padre Guillén wanted to move the mission out of the canyon about fifteen miles to the southwest for better farmland and easier access to the majority of Guaycura people. The Pericú Indian rebellion at the four southernmost missions (La Paz, Santiago, San José del Cabo, and Santa Rosa) interrupted the move until 1741. The new Los Dolores location had been a visita named La Pasión, known locally as *Tañuetía* (The Place of Ducks) or Chillá. After the move, the

Dolores mission was more typically called La Pasión, which has caused some amount of confusion with writers. Guaycura neophytes were served by Padre Guillén until 1747 when age and illness forced him to retire to Loreto. Padre Lamberto Hostell replaced Guillén at Los Dolores.

The end of Mission Los Dolores came from a bureaucratic decision rather than a site or population failure. Following the 1767 order to remove the Jesuits from their missions, Spain's Visitador General José de Gálvez ordered the mission closed in September 1768. The mission's 450 neophytes were relocated to Todos Santos, which was far outside their ancestral homeland. This made for very poor relations with both the Guaycura and the Pericú, who had lived at Todos Santos.

The Dolores Apaté site is one of Baja California's most remote and no automobile road goes to it. Visitors can take boats to the beach followed by a hike to the mission or they can take a longer, steep hike on the mission trail from the west.

The La Pasión (Los Dolores Chillá) site can be driven to in an SUV or truck on the road to Los Burros from Mexico Highway One, north of La Paz. La Pasión is located 2.5 miles east of Rancho La Presa. Only rubble from the mission walls and foundation stones remain; La Capilla is the name of the goat ranch on the mission site. Visitors are welcome.

Missionaries recorded at Los Dolores:
Jesuit
Clemente Guillén 1721-1747
(Mission moved to La Pasión in 1741)
Lamberto Hostell 1741-1743 and 1746-1768

Franciscan
Francisco Gómez April 5, 1768

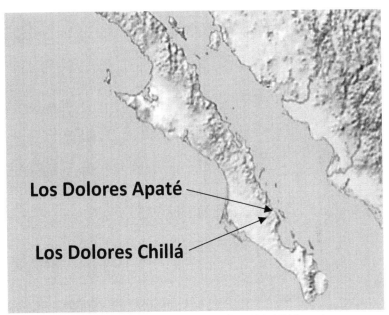

Los Dolores Apaté

Los Dolores Chillá

9) Nuestra Señora de los Dolores Apaté, 1721-1741 and Nuestra Señora de los Dolores Chillá (La Pasión), 1741-1768

"Out of the wilderness a heathen and his wife are coming with their daughters and son to the mission to be converted." Padre Ignacio Tirsch, 1762-1768.

Mission Santiago as illustrated by Ignacio Tirsch, circa 1765.

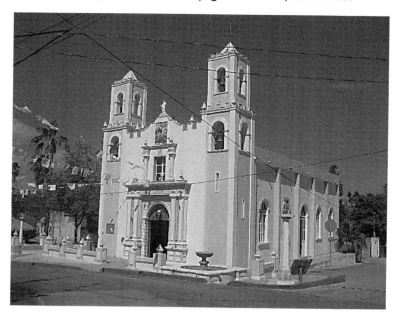

Modern church on the 1736-1795 Santiago mission site. Photo by the author in 2017.

#10 Santiago el Apóstol Aiñiní (1724-1795)

In July 1721, Padre Ignacio María Nápoli sailed south from Loreto to La Paz to begin his exploration for a new mission site between La Paz and Cabo San Lucas. Padre Jaime Bravo of the La Paz mission joined Nápoli on the expedition. The two Jesuits spent eight difficult days traveling overland to reach the gulf shore at Ensenada de las Palmas (today called Bahía de Palmas). There they believed the Cora Indians would be awaiting conversion.

After many days waiting to gain their confidence, Nápoli was confronted on the beach by a group of Indians led by a tall "sorcerer" painted with black and red stripes. This "savage" wore a cape of hair tufts and a girdle of many dangling deer hoofs. In one hand he held a fan made of feathers, in the other a bow and arrow. Gifts were presented and the Cora Indians promised to return with more "friends." Nápoli considered this first contact a success and returned to La Paz to gather supplies for a new mission. Some have called this event the founding of Mission Santiago de las Palmas or Ensenada de las Palmas. Nápoli did baptize several children before leaving for La Paz on September 8, 1721.

The trail between La Paz and Bahía de las Palmas was long and difficult. Nápoli decided a mission should first be located midway between La Paz and Ensenada de las Palmas. In 1722, Padre Nápoli began building his first mission near a place locally called Marinó, and he named the location Santa Ana. This is where Jaime Bravo's soldier, Ignacio de Rojas, had discovered silver ore two years earlier.

Two adobe rooms were built to serve as a chapel and living quarters for the padre. By 1723, Nápoli had collected enough food to feed the workforce needed to build a larger church at Santa Ana. The mission was originally named Santiago de los Coras. A storm hit the region and the people took refuge inside the unfinished church. A wall collapsed on them, killing and injuring many. The padre and his soldiers were unharmed. Relatives of those dead or wounded soon placed blame on Nápoli and the Spaniards. Padre Nápoli was forced to quit the Santiago mission project and returned to Loreto to regain his confidence and try again. Nothing remains of the Jesuit church at Santa Ana, located a few miles south of the modern town of San Antonio.

In 1724, Padre Ignacio Nápoli returned and began again to build a new mission but this time south of the Cora lands and into the land of the Pericú, at a place they called Aiñiní. Jesuit papers describing the new location were not well-known until 1973, so writers have erroneously called the new mission by the old name, Santiago de los Coras.

Aiñiní was well-watered and the new mission, now named Santiago el Apóstol, prospered for many years. In 1726, Nápoli was transferred to Sonora. His replacement was Padre Lorenzo José Carranco.

On October 1, 1734, after much unrest at the four southernmost missions, the Pericú Revolt began. Padre Carranco and two servants were killed during the uprising. An Indian named Cristóbal had been the *governor* (Indian representative) at Santiago in past years but was removed from that position after repeated shenanigans and mischief-making. Cristóbal set out to avenge himself upon Padre Carranco and took advantage of a time when there were no soldiers at Santiago or at nearby San José del Cabo.

Two days later, the Indian rebels also murdered Padre Nicolás Tamaral at San José del Cabo.

The mission was vacant for two years while the Jesuits with additional Spanish soldiers and friendly Indians regrouped. Only a few foundation stones remain today at the 1724 mission site, now located on private land.

In 1736, the mission was moved about two miles south and rebuilt. In 1748, Mission San José del Cabo was closed and became a visita of Santiago el Apóstol. San José del Cabo was later reopened as a mission by the Franciscans, in 1768. Epidemics eventually plagued Santiago, as they had the other missions, and by 1795 the mission was closed and the forty remaining neophytes were transferred to San José del Cabo. A modern church has been built on the 1736 mission site, in the town of Santiago.

V P. Lorenzo Carranco *martyrizado en la Mijsion de Santiago de los Coras* 1° de Octubre de 1734.

Martyrdom of Padre Carranco, Oct. 1, 1734.

Missionaries recorded at Santiago:
Jesuit
Ignacio Nápoli 1724-1726
Lorenzo Carranco 1726-1734
(Vacant 1734-1736, relocated 1736)

Anton Tempis 1736-1746
Karl Neumayer 1746-1747
Sigismundo Taraval 1747-1750
Bernhard Zumziel 1750-1751
Johann Bischoff 1752-1753
Francisco Badillo 1753-1759
Francisco Escalante 1759
Julián Salazar 1760-1763
Ignacio Tirsch 1763-1768

Franciscan
José Murguía April 5, 1768
Juan Antonio García Riobó 1770-1771
Francisco Villuendas 1771

Dominican
Antonio Salas and José Estévez (to 1775) May 15, 1773
Manuel García 1776-1780
Francisco Hontiyuélo 1790-1794

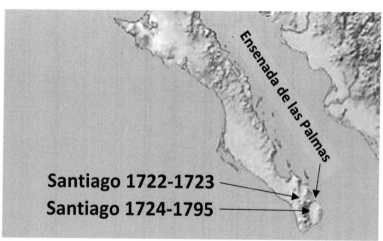

10) Santiago de los Coras, 1722-1723 and Santiago el Apóstol, 1724-1795

San Ignacio

Mission San Ignacio in 2015. Photos by the author.

Interior of San Ignacio mission church. The gold-leaf-covered altar screen (retablo) contains seven oil paintings of saints surrounding a wooden statue of San Ignacio de Loyola. Photo by the author.

#11 San Ignacio de Kadakaamán (1728-1840)

The mission of San Ignacio de Kadakaamán, was founded in 1728 by Padre Juan Bautista de Luyando, and was the eleventh Spanish mission in California. San Ignacio was the northernmost mission for the next twenty-four years and today is the northernmost Spanish mission in the state of Baja California Sur.

The site for San Ignacio was visited in 1716 by Jesuit Padre Francisco Maria Píccolo on an expedition from the mission at Mulegé. Píccolo had heard of a large settlement of Cochimí Indians and much fresh water at their home, called Kadakaamán. Once there, Píccolo found hundreds of natives awaiting conversion. Padre Píccolo named the river and location San Vicente, but that name later would be changed with the founding of the mission, twelve years later. In 1728, Padre Luyando and two soldiers first built a chapel and a house of sticks and reeds. Later those were replaced by larger rooms made of adobe and stone. Corn, wheat, olives, figs, sugarcane, pomegranate, cotton, Arabian date palms, and 500 grapevines were soon planted at San Ignacio. During 1733, Luyando's final year at San Ignacio, his grapevines produced the mission's first vintage.

Many expeditions were initiated from San Ignacio in search of new mission sites. The most famous was in 1746 and led by Padre Fernando Consag to the Colorado River Delta. This expedition finally put an end to the idea that California was an island (see map on page 212). The Jesuits now had a new directive to expand north. Santa Gertrudis, the first new mission north of San Ignacio, was founded in 1752.

Flash floods were frequently responsible for agricultural losses, so the Jesuits had massive dikes built. The largest was called a *muralla* and was three miles long, twelve feet high, and up to forty feet wide. Protective dikes had been destroyed twice before this final one was completed, in 1762. Remains of the muralla are located just east of the mission and town center of San Ignacio.

In 1765, Padre José Rotea discovered a skeleton he believed was of an eleven-foot tall man at the mission visita of San Joaquín, nine miles to the south. This firmed up the legends he heard about "giants" that lived on the peninsula before the Cochimí Indians. "Giants" was the Cochimí explanation for how the high ceiling cave art sites in the mountains north of San Ignacio were painted.

The beautiful cut-stone church of San Ignacio, whose construction was started by the Jesuits in 1761, was completed in 1786 by the Dominican Padre Juan Gómez. San Ignacio proved to be a very successful mission, remaining open until 1840 although not fully staffed after 1822. The building continued on serving as a parish church for the newly arrived Mexicans and few remaining native Californians. Today, the grand stone church is the center of the town of San Ignacio, facing the town's central plaza.

Missionaries recorded at San Ignacio:
Jesuit
Juan Luyando 1728-1733
Sebastián Sistiaga 1728-1747
Sigusmundo Taraval 1732-1733
Fernando Consag 1733-1759
Georg Retz 1751
José Rotea 1759-1768

Franciscan
Miguél de la Campa y Cos April 5, 1768
Juan de Medina Beitia 1769-1771
José Legomera 1771

Dominican
Juan Crisóstomo Gómez and José García Villatoro May 15, 1773
Joaquín Cálvo 1794-1795
Domingo Timón 1795-1798
José Loriénte 1796
Rafaél Arviña 1799-1802 and 1804-1805
José Espín 1805
Pedro Juan González 1806 and 1812-1822
Félix Caballero 1840

11) San Ignacio, 1728

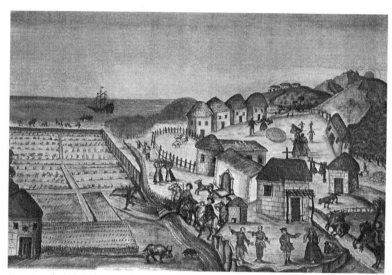

San José del Cabo as illustrated by Ignacio Tirsch circa 1765.

San José del Cabo mission ruins in a circa 1918 photo. A modern church now occupies the site, on the town plaza.

#12 San José del Cabo Añuití (1730-1748 and 1768-1840)

The next California mission was planned for the land of the Pericú. Besides the typical mission functions, it was also to provide support for the Manila Galleon, one of the original purposes for California missions. The Jesuit Visitador General, Padre José de Echeverría, chose Padre Nicolás Tamaral attending La Purísima to open the new mission.

In March 1730, Echeverría and Tamaral sailed south from Loreto to La Paz along with several Spanish soldiers. Following an inspection of the mission at La Paz, they traveled south to the visita of Todos Santos and mission of Santiago. A day's journey south from Santiago, they found a suitable site on an estuary where a fresh water river reached the sea. On April 8, 1730, San José del Cabo was founded.

Two huts were constructed of palm leaves and reeds to serve as a chapel and a house for the padre. The Pericú did not appear in the numbers anticipated until two weeks later, when Echeverría and the soldiers left. Padre Tamaral was then approached by the Indians and converted as many as a hundred in a single day. In a letter from December 1730, Tamaral wrote to Echeverría that 823 had been baptized in the eight months since the mission was founded.

Poor soil and swarms of mosquitoes forced Tamaral to move the mission further inland to a place known as Añuití.

A major issue the Jesuits had with converting the natives to Christianity was the habit of the men of having several wives. Padre Tamaral wrote of the issue to the mission's benefactor, the Marqués de Villapuente, on June 15, 1731. Tamaral describes how the wives compete with one another to gather the most food while their husbands rest all day in the shade with no need to work. Tamaral believed that only by halting polygamy was there any hope to get some work performed by the "lazy men!" Since Pericú women outnumbered men, polygamy was desired by the females for survival in the all-important family group.

It became obvious that the Jesuit imposed monogamy rule was not appreciated by the Pericú.

V. P Nicolas Tamaral. *Sevillana martyrizado en la Mission de S. Joseph del Cabo de S. Luc.* dia de N.ª del Rosario Domingo 3. de Octubre de 1734.

Martyrdom of Padre Tamaral, October 3, 1734.

The revolt of October 1734 cost the life of Tamaral and his fellow Jesuit, Padre Carranco of Mission Santiago. This mission and others of the south were destroyed as the Indians of different tribes united against the Jesuits and Spanish.

The result of the destruction of missions at Pilar de la Paz, Santiago, San José del Cabo, and Santa Rosa was that they remained deserted while the Spanish organized a response. Unknowingly, in January 1735, the Manila Galleon anchored offshore from San José del Cabo to obtain supplies after its long voyage across the Pacific. Thirteen men who came ashore in a longboat were massacred. Some Pericú men canoed out and tried to overtake the galleon, but they were repulsed and the ship weighed anchor and left for Acapulco.

The Spanish response to the uprising was carried out in February 1736 by Bernal de Huidobro, the governor of Sinaloa, with forty soldiers. They labored for a year and a half to capture all the hostile Indian leaders who were eventually banished to the mainland of Mexico. A decision was likewise made in 1736 to establish an independent military fort called the Presidio of the South at San José del Cabo.

The Presidio of the South was established at San José del Cabo in 1737 in order to station more troops in the region. Calm prevailed and rebuilding began in early 1737 when the mission of San José del Cabo was reestablished closer to the estuary near the new presidio. In 1741, the presidio was reduced in status and became an *escuadra* (sub-presidio).

Epidemics in 1742, 1744, and 1748 caused a drop in neophyte population to such a degree that in 1748 the mission of San José del Cabo was closed and it became a visita of Mission Santiago. The *Escuadra del Sur* also moved to Todos Santos in 1748. A final location change for the San José del Cabo church was made in 1753 to just north of the estuary.

On November 30, 1767, the newly appointed governor of California, Capitán Gaspar de Portolá, and twenty-five armed soldiers landed on the beach at San José del Cabo to organize the surprise removal of all Jesuits from the peninsula. Padre Ignacio Tirsch made the ride south from his mission at Santiago as the first California Jesuit to greet Portolá, not aware of the orders Potolá brought.

San José del Cabo was returned to full mission status by the Franciscans who replaced the Jesuits, in 1768. In the few months the missions were without their padres, the neophytes became demoralized, and the Franciscans had to undo damage done by the Spanish soldiers who were briefly in charge. The new Spanish inspector-general, José de Gálvez, was determined to equalize populations at the missions, and in September 1768 he ordered forty-four neophytes moved from San Javier to San José del Cabo. All but three of them died during an epidemic in 1769.

The Franciscans would soon be in charge of the new region north of the peninsula, then called Nueva (New) California. After five years, the Dominicans arrived to begin operating the existing peninsula missions of Antigua (Old) California.

In April 1795, the mission of Santiago was closed and its few remaining neophytes were relocated to San José del Cabo. In 1799, a large adobe building was erected to replace the former San José del Cabo mission church destroyed in floods of 1793. The Indian population did increase, however, to 200 by the year 1800.

The mission was sacked in 1822 when the English admiral Thomas Cochrane used Chilean ships to harass any remaining Spanish officials who had not yet surrendered to the newly independent Mexican government. This was an act of piracy as the ships were made to appear as whaling vessels. Cochrane and the Chileans also pillaged the missions at Todos Santos and Loreto. Cochrane was a British naval captain who was appointed the first admiral of the Chilean Navy in 1818 and made a major contribution to winning independence for Chile from Spain before sailing to Baja California.

Mission services to native Californians at San José del Cabo ended about 1840, but Dominican priests continued active at the church for several years to serve the new Mexican population arriving from the mainland. The last Dominican missionary to serve at San José del Cabo was Padre Gabriel González. Padre González and Padre Tomás Mansilla, the only other Baja California Dominican, left the peninsula together in February 1855. A modern church occupies the final mission site in the city of San José del Cabo.

Missionaries recorded at San José del Cabo:
Jesuit
Nicolás Tamaral 1730-1734
(Vacant 1734-1736)
Sigismundo Taraval 1736-1738 and 1741-1746
Miguel Barco 1737
Lamberto Hostell 1738-1740
Karl Neumayer 1747 and 1750-1751
(Mission closed and became a visita of Santiago 1748-1768)

Franciscan
Juan Moran April 5, 1768
Juan Antonio García Riobó 1770-1773
Francisco Villuendas 1771

Dominican
Gerónimo Soldevilla and José Lafuente May 15, 1773,
Francisco Hontiyuélo 1794
Rafael Arviña 1795-1796
Eudaldo Surroca 1797-1798
Pablo María de Zárate 1798-1821
Ignacio Ramírez 1835-1841
José de Santa Cruz 1841-1844
Gabriel Gonzáles 1846-1848

Missions founded 1730-1737

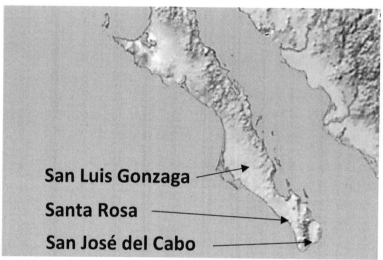

San Luis Gonzaga
Santa Rosa
San José del Cabo

12) San José del Cabo, 1730
13) Santa Rosa, 1733
14) San Luis Gonzaga, 1737

Stones possibly attributed to Mission Santa Rosa (1733-1748) and the second site of Mission Pilar de la Paz (1748-1825) at Km 49.5 on Highway 19. Photo by the author in 2017.

#13 Santa Rosa de las Palmas (1733-1748)

In 1724, Padre Jaime Bravo of the mission at La Paz became aware of the *ranchería* of Uchití natives (a Guaycura Indian group) some fifty miles to the south and two miles from the Pacific Ocean. Padre Bravo found the location excellent to farm and become a potential visita of his mission, Pilar de la Paz. Neophytes from Jesuit missions in Sinaloa were sent over to clear the land for growing. Bravo named this visita "Todos Santos" (no local native name was recorded).

By 1731, Todos Santos had become an important producer of food. When its own natives were nearly gone due to epidemics or fighting with other Indian groups, some families of Pericú Indians living further south were brought in. In 1732, the Jesuits decided to establish a separate mission at Todos Santos just as soon as funds and a priest were available.

An endowment came from Doña Rosa de la Peña, the Marquesa de las Torres (sister-in-law of the Marqués de Villapuente) to establish a new mission. It was to be named Santa Rosa in her honor. Padre Sigismundo Taraval was the founding Jesuit, opening the mission in August 1733. The visita name "Todos Santos" was the name typically used to describe the site, even after it became the Mission of Santa Rosa de las Palmas.

Some confusion on the location of Mission Santa Rosa appears on old maps and in letters, describing the mission as being on the Bay of Las Palmas, which is on the opposite coast of the peninsula. A visita named "Santa Rosa" belonging to and just north of San José del Cabo likely contributed to the confusion.

Mission Santa Rosa was open barely a year when the Pericú Revolt broke out in October 1734. Padre Taraval was practically dragged away by the soldiers attending him when word came that his Jesuit brothers in Santiago and San José del Cabo had been murdered. Taraval had good Indian relationships and thought he could pacify the rebels if he was allowed to remain. The four southernmost missions were destroyed. Taraval would later learn that the rebels killed forty-nine women and children at his mission.

Jesuits began to return to the southern missions after more than two years of fighting between Spanish soldiers and Indian rebels. As a result of the revolt, Spanish soldiers were permanently based in the south with ten each at La Paz, Santiago, and San José del Cabo.

In 1745, King Philip V ordered an increase in the number of settlements in California coupled with a desire to expand northward.

By 1748, it was decided that the missions of the south could be consolidated from four to two. First, by closing the mission at La Paz Bay and moving it south to take over functions at Todos Santos and also closing the mission of San José del Cabo. The Escuadra del Sur (a sub-presidio of Spanish soldiers) was also moved to Todos Santos from San José del Cabo.

In 1748, the Mission of Pilar de la Paz relocated to Todos Santos and the mission enterprise there, named Santa Rosa de las Palmas, came to an end. While the mission name was changed to Nuestra Señora del Pilar de la Paz, the location and mission typically continued to be called Todos Santos. In 1825, the Pilar de la Paz mission moved a second time, one-mile south to where the church now is, in the town plaza.

One visita of the mission was named San Jacinto and is about fifteen miles to the southeast. Adobe ruins survived into the twenty-first century at San Jacinto.

The original Todos Santos mission site has become a playground along Highway 19, in front of a church that was built in 1970. See also the chapter on Mission #7, Pilar de la Paz, page 57.

Jesuit Missionaries recorded at Santa Rosa:
Sigusmundo Taraval 1733-1734
(Vacant 1734-1736)
Bernhard Zumziel 1737-1748

Visita San Jacinto ruins in 2002. Photo by Jack Swords.

Mission San Luis Gonzaga in 2017. Photo by the author.

Mission San Luis Gonzaga in 1951. Photo by Howard Gulick.

#14 San Luis Gonzaga Chiriyaqui (1737-1768)

Mission San Luis Gonzaga is on the Magdalena Plain of Baja California Sur. In 1721, it was originally established as a visita, or satellite visiting chapel of the mission of Los Dolores Apaté. The Guaycura Indian name for the oasis was Chiriyaqui (Chiriyaki). On July 14, 1737, the visita was elevated to mission status with the arrival of Jesuit Padre Lamberto (Lambert) Hostell. The mission was named after Don Luis de Velasco, who provided 10,000 pesos for its founding. This mission was usually referred to simply as "San Luis" in most letters and reports of the time. San Luis Gonzaga was the last mission founded in the southern half of the peninsula, today's state of Baja California Sur.

Padre Hostell was not able to remain at his new mission after its founding because he was called away to an emergency at San José del Cabo. His time away lasted from August 1737 to November 1740. Hostell returned to San Luis Gonzaga after that absence of over two years.

The Guaycura tribes of the Magdalena Plain were scattered to such a degree that Hostell's first order of business was to establish three *pueblos* (population centers) that included his mission plus two visitas. One visita was called San Juan Nepomuceno and the other was called Santa María Magdalena on the bay of the same name. A third visita was planned and was to be called Santa Trinidad, but records do not indicate it was established. In addition to attending his own mission, Hostell would travel frequently to Los Dolores and assist Padre Guillén.

In 1744, the Visitador General of the Jesuits was Padre Juan Antonio Balthasar and as part of his duties, he made a routine tour of the California missions. He reported the neophyte population at San Luis as being 488. Balthasar also noted that

Padre Hostell was attempting to establish a mission at the visita of Magdalena. Balthasar suggested to his superiors that a new missionary be sent to assist Hostell to open a Magdalena mission. An additional Jesuit in California would also allow Hostell to assist his old companion Padre Clemente Guillén at Los Dolores. This proposed mission on the great Pacific bay never materialized. Padre Hostell was later sent to Los Dolores and replaced an ill and dying Padre Guillén. Padre Juan Javier Bischoff replaced Hostell at San Luis Gonzaga from 1746 to early 1751.

Padre Jacobo (Johann Jakob) Baegert arrived on May 28, 1751 and remained at San Luis Gonzaga for seventeen years. When Baegert arrived, he found the site in a somewhat ruined condition. Bischoff had left sometime before Baegert arrived, and in the interim a storm collapsed the small church there. Two other huts were all that stood at the mission to serve for storage and a residence. The new padre began to remodel his house by adding windows to let in light, a tiled roof, and to whitewash the walls. It had been such a dark room, Baegert called it a "cave."

The handsome cut-stone church that remains intact to this day was constructed from March 1753 until December 1758. Baegert had an aqueduct constructed from the mission spring to a small plot where he planted cabbage, melons, turnips, and sugarcane. Later he planted wheat and corn, but the water was limited and the dry climate restricted production. Plagues of locusts also frequently destroyed crops. The desert surrounding the mission provided great quantities of the pitahaya cactus fruit. Baegert would sometimes serve himself pitahayas with wine poured over them, on a china plate, and pretend he was eating strawberries back in Germany. Goats, sheep, and cattle were raised at the mission along with horses and mules.

94

Baegert and his Jesuit brothers were all forced to leave their missions and return to Europe by Royal Order of King Carlos III. The sixteen Jesuits all left California soil on February 3, 1768. Baegert wrote a most detailed account of his mission experiences and of the native Californians and it was published in 1772. An English translation was published in 1952 under the title, *Observations in Lower California* (see map on page 213).

When the Franciscans assumed operations of the California missions in April 1768, a report gave the population of San Luis Gonzaga at 310. Padre Andrés Villaumbrales was the new Franciscan missionary at San Luis Gonzaga. However, Villaumbrales was not there long before his mission was closed. Spain's new Visitador General, José de Gálvez decided to populate the rich agricultural lands of Todos Santos, far to the south, with the neophytes of San Luis Gonzaga and Los Dolores. On August 20, 1768, San Luis Gonzaga mission was abandoned and its neophyte Indians joined those of nearby Dolores in a forced relocation, far from their ancestral homeland. Losing their Jesuit priests was difficult enough, but leaving their native territory was a devastating blow to the Guaycura Indians.

To visit the mission of San Luis Gonzaga, take a twenty-two-mile-long graded dirt road east from Highway One, beginning at Km 195, about eight miles south of Ciudad Constitución. A small village is located at the mission oasis. Ruins of other buildings date back to the years when this was a large cattle ranch and a rest stop on the Camino Real to La Paz.

Missionaries recorded at San Luis Gonzaga:
Jesuit
Lambert Hostell 1737-1738 and 1741-1745
Clemente Guillén 1739-1740
Johann Bischoff 1746-1750
Jakob Baegert 1751-1768

Franciscan
Andrés Villaumbrales April 5, 1768

Mulegé to Santa Gertrudis on El Camino Real, as illustrated on this 1864 map published by A. Gensoul of San Francisco, California.

Santa Gertrudis

Bells of Mission Santa Gertrudis. Photo by the author.

Mission Santa Gertrudis in 2017. Photo by the author.

Church interior, facing north. Photo by A.N. Muia.

North side exterior with Elizabeth Kier in 2012.

#15 Santa Gertrudis (1752-1822)

Fifteen years passed before the Jesuits were able to establish another mission, and it would be the first one in the northern half of the California peninsula. Padre Fernando Consag had made expeditions seeking potential mission sites, and was baptizing natives in advance, for the next mission.

The first expedition was in June 1746 traveling in four small sail boats. They traveled along the gulf coast from San Carlos (a small inlet northeast of San Ignacio) to the mouth of the Colorado River. This expedition once again confirmed that California was not an island. Other Jesuits, including Padres Ugarte and Kino, had found this to be the case years before on their expeditions to the north though their views were not widely accepted. Consag's findings convinced his superiors to connect the missions of California with those in Sonora on the Mexican mainland, so a push to build north was finally made. A land route of communication would be preferred over crossing the often violent waters of the Gulf of California. Additionally, more Californians would be Christianized and civilized for the King.

The second Consag expedition was by land in May 1751. It began north of San Ignacio at a place with a small stream that Consag had visited before and named La Piedad. They traveled northwest nearly to Punta Baja (near today's El Rosario) before returning. Consag found no place that offered any better site for a new mission than did La Piedad. Padre Consag baptized over 500 Indians in 1751 and assigned them to the proposed future mission. The new mission's official name was to be Dolores del Norte. That name appeared on maps and Jesuit reports dating back to 1744, but at that early date, Dolores del Norte was a mission only on paper. This caused some writers in the 20th century to believe a lost mission existed with that name. Some, including *INAH* (*Instituto Nacional de Anthropolgía e Historia*), Mexico's National Institute of Anthropology and History, have also called the large visita ruins in San Pablo Canyon, "Mission Dolores del Norte," in error.

Consag began preparing the La Piedad site with the help of a highly skilled but blind Cochimí Indian named Andrés Comanají. Comanají took the name "Sistiaga" out of affection for his former teacher (Padre Sebastián de Sistiaga) at Mulegé. Andrés Comanají Sistiaga managed the construction at La Piedad for the future mission. Its official founding would occur once a new priest was available and ready.

The name of the new mission was changed to Santa Gertrudis out of respect for the benefactor, Don José de la Puente Peña, the Marqués de Villapuente, in honor of his wife, Gertrudis de la Peña. He had funded the mission at San José del Cabo but left instructions that if that mission was ever abandoned, his money was to be used to establish a mission in the land of the Cochimí. Mission San José del Cabo was closed by the Jesuits in 1748 thus the transfer of financial support occurred.

Padre Georg Retz opened Santa Gertrudis on July 15, 1752, following a year of training at San Ignacio where he learned the Cochimí language. Hundreds and hundreds of Cochimí came to be baptized and join the mission. Desiring this mission to be self-sufficient, Padre Retz had ditches dug into solid rock to transport water from the spring to fields he had cleared and filled with soil. Wheat and corn grew and was harvested. Eventually the vineyards produced mission wine in tanks created by hollowing boulders, as wooden casks were not available. Figs, peaches, pomegranates, and olives grew in the mission orchards. Livestock was raised. Retz had created a mission-oasis in the center of the peninsula's desert. Neophytes numbering 1,730 were reported at Mission Santa Gertrudis in 1762, ten years after it was founded.

In 1768, the Jesuits were removed from California and replaced by the Franciscans. Padre Dionisio Basterra was placed in charge of about 1,360 neophytes at Santa Gertrudis. Spain's Visitador General José de Gálvez ordered some of the Santa Gertrudis neophytes south to populate missions needing labor for their farmlands.

In 1773, the Dominicans arrived to take over the mission operations in Old (or Lower) California, and the Franciscans were to only operate missions in New (or Upper) California. By 1782, the population at Santa Gertrudis had dropped to 317. A cut-stone mission church completed in 1796 replaced the earlier adobe one. In 1800, the population at the mission was down to 203 as epidemics took their toll.

One large mission visita is located about twenty-five miles south, in San Pablo Canyon, a site sometimes misnamed "Dolores del Norte." Visita de San Pablo is located east of the town of Vizcaíno and today can be reached by trail, using a guide, as it is located inside a protected archeological zone.

Mission Santa Gertrudis is located just north of the border between the states of Baja California and Baja California Sur, twenty-three miles east of El Arco on a graded dirt road. The twenty-five-mile unpaved highway to El Arco begins at Highway One (Km 189), seventeen miles southbound from Guerrero Negro. Another route is thirty-seven miles from Highway One (Km 154), starting about seven miles north of the town of Vizcaíno, and passes through the abandoned village of Guillermo Prieto. Cars with low ground clearance are not recommended on any back-country roads.

Missionaries recorded at Santa Gertrudis:
Jesuit
Georg Retz 1752-1768

Franciscan
Dionisio Basterra April 5, 1768
Juan Sancho de la Torre 1770
Gregorio Amurrio 1771-1773

Dominican
Manuel Rodríguez and José Díez Bustamante (to 1777) May 15, 1773
Juan Antonio Formoso 1783
Joaquín Valero 1788
José Espín 1794-1798
Segismundo Foncubierta 1812

Visita San Pablo, often mistaken for a proposed mission named Dolores del Norte. Photo by Phil Lang in 2010.

Map of the Northern Jesuit Mission Sites

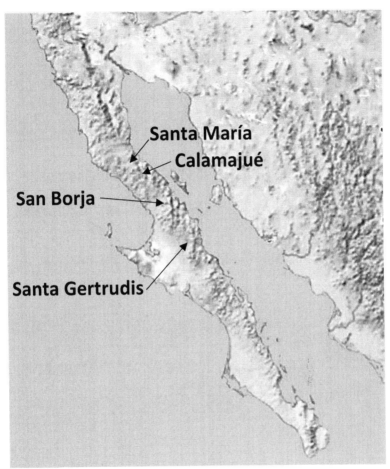

15) Santa Gertrudis, 1752
16) San Borja, 1762
17a) Calamajué, 1766
17b) Santa María, 1767

Adobe church ruins at San Borja from Jesuit and Franciscan period. An awning erected in 2001 now protects part of these ruins.

Stone church at San Borja from the Dominican period. Photos by Jack Swords.

#16 San Francisco de Borja Adac (1762-1818)

The Jesuits had decided to expand their missions northward after Fernando Consag's sea voyage in 1746 proved that California was not an island. Yet nearly twenty years later, the island versus peninsula issue was still being debated. A chain of missions north from San Ignacio and around the Gulf of California to the missions in Sonora was started in 1752 with the founding of Mission Santa Gertrudis. The Jesuits were removed from the New World before the missions on both sides of the gulf could be connected and the impetus for that plan ended as well.

Land expeditions by Padre Consag in 1751 and again in 1753 failed to find an acceptable site for the next mission to be established to the north. Padre Georg Retz of Santa Gertrudis then began to send his neophytes out in search of possible mission sites. By 1758, Padre Retz learned of some hot springs called Adac by the Cochimí Indians. The water smelled of sulfur, but once it cooled it could be drunk without ill effect. Adac was nearly a three-day journey from Santa Gertrudis but relatively close to the fine natural harbor of Bahía de los Ángeles, some twelve hours by trail away. Supplies and personnel could be offloaded at that bay to support the new mission.

In 1758, Fernando Consag was promoted to Padre Visitador of the California Jesuits, and it was Consag, who desired to establish a new mission at Adac. However, Consag died in 1759 before seeing the project get under way. New mission funds were provided by an inheritance to the Jesuits from the Duchess of Gandía, Doña María de Borja (of the respected Borgia family in Spain). The inheritance became available in 1747 but was delivered to California in 1756.

In advance of the new mission's founding, Padre Retz had a road built to Adac and began construction there. The site became a visita of Santa Gertrudis on August 27, 1759. Padre José Rotea was chosen the new priest in charge, but when Padre Consag died, Rotea filled the vacancy created at San Ignacio. Padre Retz continued working at Adac where he had built a church, living quarters, a warehouse, and a hospital. Corn was planted in a small field by the hot spring. Retz had also baptized 300 Cochimí Indians for the new center.

Padre Wenceslaus Linck arrived in California and spent a few months with Georg Retz at Santa Gertrudis learning the Cochimí language. Linck then rode north and arrived at his new post on September 1, 1762. In honor of the benefactor, the new mission was named San Francisco de Borja for the saint and Duchess María's ancestor. Additional baptisms numbering 142 were added during the mission's first month of service. Supplies were shipped from Loreto to Bahía de los Ángeles, where a large Cochimí ranchería was located. The natives were able to provide overland transport to San Borja, twenty-six miles by trail from the bay.

The first snow Europeans observed in California was witnessed in December 1763 at Las Cabras. Located fourteen miles south of San Borja and over 4,200 feet in elevation, Las Cabras is where the mission's cattle were brought to graze. By 1764 the mission's neophyte population exceeded 1,000. Padre Linck got assistance with the arrival of Padre Victoriano Arnés who came to train under Linck and learn the Cochimí dialect. This training was also required in advance of Arnés establishing the next mission to the north. The population of Mission San Borja swelled to 1,700 neophytes by the end of 1766. Another Jesuit, Padre Juan José Díez, arrived to assist Linck and Arnés.

The neophytes could not all stay at San Borja as not enough food was produced there to sustain such a population. About thirty to forty Indian families could live at the mission itself and others would come from their rancherías on rotation for instruction. The mission *pueblos* (visitas or rancherías) of Los Ángeles and Guadalupe were on the gulf coast; San Ignacio (San Ignacito today) and El Rosario (Rosarito today) were to the west; Santa Ana, San Miguel, and San Régis were to the south; and another called San Juan was included in a 1772 report. Further south is the canyon and ranch of El Paraiso, listed as a mission farm. Nine miles southeast of San Borja is the abandoned adobe ranch house of San Gregorio. It is built on large cut-stones, seemingly indicative of mission-era construction.

Linck made two major expeditions out from San Borja in search of even more converts. One was in 1765 to the island of Ángel de la Guarda in the Gulf of California where fires had been seen on the island and reported to Linck. Using the mission's launch, they reached the island but after considerable exploration found no trace of human activity or sources of fresh water. The second expedition would take the Jesuit far north to pine-covered mountains and within sight of the Colorado River Delta. That expedition began on February 20, 1766, with thirteen soldiers and several Indians. For almost two months, Padre Linck explored up the center of the peninsula. Linck's discoveries included a future mission site named Velicatá by the Indians.

The Franciscan Order replaced the Jesuits in 1768 and operated the California peninsula missions until mid-1773 when they divided California mission duties with the Dominican Order. Padre Fermín Francisco de Lasuén was the Franciscan priest stationed at San Borja. In 1773 he reported San Borja as having a new adobe church measuring ninety-one feet by twenty-two feet, with a roof of palm leaves. The Mission San Borja Indian population had dropped to 1,000 that year, as the people succumbed to diseases and forced lifestyle changes.

In 1801, construction was reported as being nearly completed on the large cut-stone church. Sadly, the Indian population had continued to drop and was below 400. No missionary letters or reports are known to exist after 1816. The Mexican War of Independence ran from 1810 through 1821 and contact between California and Spain was minimal at best. The war and rapidly declining Indian population spelled an end to San Borja and the other Spanish missions.

San Borja is the furthest north stone mission church on the California peninsula. Two graded dirt roads connect to San Borja, one from the Bahia de los Ángeles highway (Km 45) and the other from Highway One at Rosarito (Km 52). Both roads are just over twenty miles in length and best driven in an SUV or truck. The sight of this Spanish church in the center of Baja California is well worth the effort it takes to get there.

Missionaries recorded at San Borja:
Jesuit
Wenceslaus Linck 1762-1768
Victoriano Arnés 1764-1766
Juan Díez 1765-1766

Franciscan
Francisco de Lasuén April 5, 1768
Andrés Villaumbrales 1769
Juan Figuer 1771

Dominican

Manuel García (to 1775) and José Aivár (to 1776) May 15, 1773
Luis Sáles 1778-1781
Antonio Caballero 1792-1794
Rafaél Caballero 1792-1794
Martín Zavaleta 1793
Mélchor Pons 1794, 1797-1798 and 1803
Juan María Salgado 1795-1796
Antonio Lázaro 1797-1798 and 1802
Tomás de Ahumada 1805-1809
Ramón de Santos 1812
José Martín 1812-1816

Calamajué/ Santa María

Mission site at Calamajué in 2012. Photo by the author.

Mission Santa María in 1961. Photo by Howard Gulick.

Mission Santa María in 2010. Photo by the author.

#17 Nuestra Señora de Columna (Calamajué) /Santa María de los Ángeles (1766-1775)

The seventeenth Jesuit California mission was founded by Padre Victoriano Arnés and Padre Juan José Díez. The first mission location was at a site named Calagnujuet. The Cochimí name was soon modified to Calamajué ("Calah-mah-WAY"). Johann Jakob Baegert's 1772 book, *Observations in Lower California*, provides the founding name of the mission as Nuestra Señora de Columna. "Columna" also appears on a map in the original German edition of Baegert's book. Typically, this mission was called Calamajué. Some historians consider Calamajué as only a visita of Mission San Borja, but the documents show otherwise.

The running stream at Calamajué was discovered by Padre Fernando Consag in 1753 on his third expedition and revisited by Padre Wenceslaus Linck on April 12, 1766. During his 1766 expedition, Linck had discovered a fine site for a future mission far north, the location was called Velicatá by the Cochimí Indians. The distance to Velicatá from Mission San Borja was too great through a potentially hostile region, and Calamajué was the only possible place for a mission known to the Jesuits between the two. Using funds provided by the *Duquesa* (Duchess) of Gandía, Doña María de Borja (of the famous Borgia family in Spain), the Jesuit Padre Visitador Lamberto Hostell, gave the order for a mission at Calamajué to be founded.

On October 16, 1766, Arnés and Díez arrived at the site after traveling for two days from San Borja with ten soldiers and fifty neophytes. The Calamajué site is on a shelf at the edge of a broad arroyo where a year-round stream emerges from a canyon. The water is heavily mineralized and undrinkable, although the local Cochimí natives were known to have survived on it. Wells had to be dug more than a mile away to provide potable water for the mission. The padres had hoped the minerals in the stream would serve as fertilizer for crops they would plant.

Soon construction of an adobe chapel, a storehouse, and residence for the missionaries was begun. Shacks were made for the soldiers' quarters. Only one wooden door was available and it was used to secure the storehouse. In the first months at the new mission, 200 Indians were baptized. Not long after the founding, Padre Díez became quite ill and returned to San Borja. Arnés continued on at Calamajué without Díez and soon had a confrontation with a tribe from a place called Cagnajuet seventy miles north.

The men of Cagnajuet became angry when young women from their ranchería joined the mission. The men of Cagnajuet conspired with the Cochimí at Velicatá to kill the missionaries and soldiers. The Velicatá Cochimí had remembered the kindness of Padre Linck several months earlier and wanted no part in bringing harm to the Spanish. Juan Nepomuceno was the Cochimí neophyte governor at Calamajué. He sent six well-armed neophytes to Cagnajuet, captured the troublemakers, and brought them to the mission. Padre Arnés interceded and spared the prisoners from the lash, thus gaining their friendship and converting them to becoming Christians.

Wheat was planted, but when irrigated with the Arroyo Calamajué water, it withered and died. The soil became white with the salts from the stream. The mission could not survive any longer at Calamajué and seven months after Mission Nuestra Señora de Columna was founded, Padre Victoriano Arnés discovered a better location with good water. It was thirty miles away and called (in the Cochimí language) Cabujakaamang. There was not much arable land on which to cultivate crops, but the fine bay of San Luis Gonzaga was nearby and it was reasoned that seafood could supplement their diet. Supplies from the south and mainland of Mexico could be also be offloaded there.

The mission was relocated in May 1767 to Cabujakaamang and renamed Santa María de los Ángeles. When missions were moved, a complete name change was rare. This may have led to some confusion with writers about the relationship between Calamajué and Santa María. These both were indeed one mission, but two locations. The renamed and reestablished mission was to be a new start. What actually resulted would turn out to be the last mission center founded by the Jesuits. Orders for the Jesuits expulsion from the New World had already been made and were in route to Mexico from Spain during this period.

The new site had limited resources but palms provided wood for building shacks that served as a chapel and residence for the missionary and his soldiers. Wheat and cotton were planted and in good condition when the expulsion orders arrived in January 1768. Santa María had 300 neophytes (baptized Indians) and thirty *catechumen* (Indians preparing for baptism) at the time of the expulsion.

Almost four months had passed following the removal of the Jesuits before the Franciscans arrived to resume mission functions. Padre Juan Leon de Medina Beitia (also spelled Beytia or Veitia) arrived in May 1768. He saw that Santa María was lacking a suitable church, so he had one erected from adobe and roofed with tules (reeds). Next to it, a two-room adobe dwelling was constructed as well as a barn that served as a storage room.

After almost a year of isolation coupled with a lack of provisions here at Santa María, Padre Beitia removed himself to Mission San Ignacio by April 14, 1769. To fill the void at Santa María, San Borja's Padre Fermin Francisco de Lausen, traveled to Santa María. Padre Andrés Villumbrales had been assigned to Mission San Luis Gonzaga, but when it was closed he was sent to San Borja to assist Lausen who was dividing his time between two missions.

California Franciscan President Junípero Serra, during his expedition to Alta California, was at Santa María from May 5 to May 11, 1769. Serra examined the lonely mission and found it had potential greater than the reports he had read. Serra's opinion to further develop Santa María changed, however, after he arrived at Velicatá, three days later. It was on May 14, 1769 that Serra founded Mission San Fernando at Velicatá.

Serra had a cargo trail constructed from San Luis Gonzaga Bay to San Fernando, passing just north of Santa María's valley. The Camino Real route was also improved between Calamajué and Santa María by moving it from the bottom of the deep canyon, east of the mission, and placing it on top of the north rim of the canyon.

The highest population recorded at Mission Santa María was 523 in September 1771. Five families and four single young men lived at the mission center and the others lived in various rancherías surrounding the mission. In a report from February 12, 1772, Padre Francisco Palóu states that Mission Santa María loaned one of its bells to Mission San Fernando de Velicatá to serve that new mission's needs. In 1772, an unnamed epidemic caused the population to drop, and just 317 neophytes where living in the Santa María territory in 1773. In 1774, a final census at Mission Santa María recorded 485 neophytes. By 1775 the mission's neophytes were relocated to Mission San Fernando and Santa María became just an outpost on El Camino Real.

At the first mission site (Calamajué) only the outlines of the adobe walled church and other buildings remain today. Calamajué is accessed on a dirt road, east and then south thirteen miles from Coco's Corner (a road junction located off Highway Five, thirteen miles north of Laguna Chapala and twenty-three miles south of Bahía San Luis Gonzaga).

The adobe ruins at Santa María are most impressive, perhaps because of its remoteness and dry climate. The 14.5 mile "extreme" dirt road to Santa María begins at Rancho Santa Ynez (just south of Cataviña, off Highway One, Km 181) and is known as one of the roughest four-wheel drive trails in Baja California. Less than two miles from the mission is a steep, rocky grade known as the "widowmaker" followed by a swamp with water levels sometimes two feet deep referred to as the "bog". The mission is just over a ridge from the bog. The final half mile has steep gullies as a final barrier to many vehicles.

Missionaries recorded at Calamajué/Santa María:
Jesuit
Juan Díez 1766
Victoriano Arnés 1766-1768
(Mission moved and renamed in 1767)

Franciscan
Juan de Medina Beitia April 5, 1768
Francisco de Lasuén 1769 (from San Borja)
Miguél de la Campa y Cos 1769-1773 (from San Fernando)
Antonio Linares 1771 (from San Fernando)
Vicente Fuster 1771-1773 (from San Fernando)

Dominican
Miguel Hidalgo (to 1774) and Pedro Gandiága (to 1774) May 15, 1773

San Fernando mission in 1926. Photo by George Hendry.

San Fernando mission ruins in 1974. Photo by the author.

San Fernando ruins in 2017. Photo by the author.

#18 San Fernando de Velicatá (1769-1822)

As it had been firmly established that California was a peninsula, Spain wanted to expand north to prevent the Russians or British from claiming the land that was now proven to be contiguous to the north. Beginning in 1769, the peninsula was known as Antigua (Old) California, and the land from San Diego north was called Nueva (New) California. Later, the names changed to Baja California and Alta California. However, the two Californias did not become separate political districts until March 26, 1804.

The next California mission site beyond Santa María was called Velicatá by the Cochimí natives and was discovered on March 5, 1766, by the Jesuit missionary Padre Wenceslaus Linck while exploring for new mission locations. Velicatá was ideal with plenty of good water and friendly Indians to baptize. Before the Jesuits could establish a mission there, they were removed from the New World by orders of Spain's King Carlos III. The sixteen Jesuits in California left in February

1768 and were replaced by the Franciscans, who arrived two months later.

The Franciscans were under the authority of the Spanish government and without the special conditions that the Jesuits had arranged. The Franciscans, and the Dominicans who followed, seemed less interested in native language skills. They also did not allow the Indians as much freedom to move about as had the Jesuits.

During his trek north from Loreto to establish missions in Alta California, Junípero Serra founded his first California mission at Velicatá. This was on May 14, 1769, and Serra named the new mission San Fernando. This was the first California mission founded by the Franciscan Order, and it was also the only mission founded by Franciscans on the peninsula. As Serra was to continue north to San Diego, he placed Padre Miguel de la Campa y Cos in charge of the new mission, who baptized some 390 Indians. Livestock and farming were productive thanks to the construction of a dam and irrigation canals. In February 1772, Padres Antonio Linares and Vicente Fuster relieved Campo y Cos at San Fernando.

On recognizing the potential of Alta California, the Franciscans relented to the Dominican's request to share mission duties in California. The Dominicans were to operate all the active missions founded by the Jesuits plus the one Franciscan mission founded at Velicatá (San Fernando). They were also to establish five new missions between San Fernando and San Diego.

After just five years, the Franciscans handed over Mission San Fernando and the other thirteen active Baja California missions to the Dominicans. This was indeed far more than the Dominicans had bargained for, and only later did they discover why the Franciscans so readily gave up the peninsula missions. The southern peninsula missions were in decline. Epidemics and a total disruption of Native Californian life had doomed their future.

In July 1773, San Fernando was transferred to the Dominicans. The mission had a church and a priest's dwelling both made of adobe and covered with tules (reeds). The new Dominican priest assigned to San Fernando was Miguel Hidalgo and he was assisted by Padre Pedro Gandiága. Gandiága served San Fernando mission for the next seventeen years. Friction arose between the Franciscans and Dominicans at San Fernando when the Franciscans insisted on taking the Baja California mission possessions with them to Alta California, including food that the Dominicans needed to feed the neophytes there at San Fernando.

Between 1774 and 1775, 500 natives were baptized by Padres Hidalgo and Gandiága. In 1775, the mission of Santa María was closed and its neophytes transferred to San Fernando, increasing San Fernando's population to 1,406. In the next seven years, the population of San Fernando mission dropped to 642 as epidemics took their toll. The 1782 mission livestock report shows that it had 110 head of cattle, 178 sheep, 65 goats, and 31 mules and horses. The mission farm produced 615 bushels of wheat, 685 bushels of corn, and 178 bushels of barley. A small amount of cotton was also grown.

Many other Dominicans also served at San Fernando over the following years. The mission books have survived into modern times and many details were saved.

The adobe church building was about eighty-five feet by sixteen feet when reported in 1793. In 1798, an additional adobe building measuring forty-five feet by twenty feet was erected for storage.

Padre Antonio Lázaro served from March 1799 to December 1804 and in those five years baptized only thirty-two native Indians. The mortality rate from smallpox, measles, syphilis, and the "European style of living" for the Cochimí natives far outpaced their birth rate. Antonio Lázaro was replaced by Padre Manuel del Aguila (1804-1806). Padre Aguila had seen a neophyte population of 295 dwindle to 201 in his two years. By 1814 fewer than one-hundred native converts were counted as residing at or near San Fernando.

Entries into the record book were made by several other priests between the years 1808 and 1825. The exact date of abandonment is not clear, but we can determine from the book of records that the final marriage was on October 3, 1814, by Padre Bernardo Solá. The final baptism entry was on June 21, 1818, by Padre José Martín. The final death notice was entered into the mission book on October 19, 1821, by Padre Francisco Troncoso. The last entry in San Fernando's book of records was on May 16, 1825, for the visitation of Padres Domingo Luna and Félix Caballero.

A visita of San Fernando was located fifteen miles north, at San Juan de Dios. In 2006, a farmer clearing and plowing the desert destroyed the adobe ruins at San Juan de Dios. This happened despite its being a historic site documented by INAH. In 2017, some of the ruins had been uncovered. San Juan de Dios is twenty-two unpaved miles northeast of Highway One, leaving the highway near Km 103. See the photo from 2000 on page 204.

Mission San Fernando is reached just over two miles west from Highway One at the junction to El Progreso, Km 121. The dirt road is passable to most vehicles. El Progreso is thirty-nine miles from El Rosario's gas station (Km 57).

Missionaries recorded at San Fernando:
Franciscan
Junípero Serra May 14, 1769
Miguél de la Campa y Cos 1769-1773
Antonio Linares 1771
Vicente Fuster 1771-1773

Dominican
Miguel Hidalgo (to 1777) and Pedro Gandiága (to 1790) May 15, 1773
Francisco Galistéo 1773-1774
Manuel García 1775
Manuel Pérez 1775, 1778, 1780, and 1782
José Díez Bustamante 1778
Antonio Luésma 1782-1783
Juan Antonio Formoso 1785-1788
Pedro de Acebedo (Azevedo) 1788-1789
Miguel Abád 1789
Tomás Marín 1789
Jórge Coéllo 1790-1795
Mariano Apolinário 1795
Rafaél Arviña 1796-1799
Vicente Belda 1797-1798
José Caulas 1797-1798
Jaime Codina 1798
Antonio Lázaro 1799-1804
Segismundo Fontcubierta 1800 and 1802
Pedro González 1804
José Portela 1804

Manuel de Aguila 1804-1806
José Duro 1807-1808
Ramón de Santos 1808-1813
Bernardo Solá 1811-1814
Tomás de Ahumada 1815
Antonio Menéndez 1815 and 1822-1825 (from San Vicente)
José Martín 1816-1818
Francisco Troncoso 1819-1822 (from El Rosario)

El Rosario

El Rosario 1774 site ruins in 2005. Photo by the author, facing south.

Facing west from the same point as the previous image. Photo by the author.

El Rosario 1774 mission site ruins in 2017. Photo by the author.

El Rosario 1802 mission ruins in 2017. Photo by the author.

El Rosario 1802 mission site ruins in 2011. Photo by the author.

#19 Nuestra Señora del Rosario de Viñadaco (1774-1822)

El Rosario was the first California mission founded by the Dominican Order, just a year after assuming responsibility for over a dozen Jesuit-founded missions and one mission founded by the Franciscans. The site for El Rosario was known to the Cochimí Indians as Viñadaco (also spelled Viñaraco or Viñatacót). The valley was investigated by Dominican President Padre Vicente Mora in late 1773. He found fresh water pools, and after digging some wells, tapped into a flowing spring of water. The first mission location is on the north side of the river valley and five miles from the ocean. No better location for a mission was found at the time than this one at Viñadaco.

Padre Francisco Galistéo founded the mission on July 24, 1774, after he had already begun priestly duties, such as performing a marriage three days earlier.

Padre Galistéo served at El Rosario until the end of 1779. However, he had assistance from Padres Manuel Hidalgo, Manuel Pérez, José Aivár, and Pedro Gandiága. Padre Luis Sáles also performed baptisms in 1778. Padre Sáles was the only Dominican to have his letters published in a book, *Observations on California, 1772-1790*.

In 1790, Padre Luis Sáles wrote the following:

"In the year 1774 we were given an order to explore some territories in which to found new settlements and to establish the conquest of the heathen, and this in spite of the fact that the Franciscans had explored the locations indicated by the King and reported them as useless. Nevertheless, whether because of rains or the freshets of the arroyos, or other circumstances which I omit, a place with many heathen, called Viñatacót, was found, which served for the foundation of a mission named Nuestra Señora del Rosario, and it has turned out so prosperous that today it is one of the richest settlements, supplying much grain to maintain the neighboring Indians."

Several Dominicans entered their names in the mission record books of El Rosario, and the books, which recorded baptisms, marriages, and deaths, have been preserved into modern times. A report in 1793 describes the church constructed of adobe one-hundred-thirty feet by twenty-five feet in size. There was also a room for the priests to reside in. A room twenty-two feet long was added in 1798. In 1800, four rooms were added for storage, weaving, a kitchen, and a forge; all were made of adobe.

The neophyte population numbers at El Rosario was reported as being 564 in 1776, after which epidemics took their toll dropping the population to 251 in 1782. An increase to 390 was reported in 1793, then a drop to 257 in 1800, 199 in 1808, and just 38 in 1829.

In 1802 the mission was moved two miles west and closer to the river, after the spring dried up at the first site. One story says that the spring was buried by a flood-caused landslide. The first site is locally referred to as El Rosario de Arriba (Upper Rosario), the second site as El Rosario de Abajo (Lower Rosario). The second site had been an Indian ranchería named San José. A multi-room adobe building was erected at San José in 1799. The second mission location was not only closer to the river but also closer to the ocean and had more land available for cultivation. The new mission church was made of massive earthen walls on a foundation of mortared stones. The doorway was a pointed Gothic arch, something unseen at other California missions built in the same period. The walls were coated with white plaster that would have been brilliant and visible from great distances. The El Rosario mission was perhaps the most stable and successful of the Dominican missions.

The date the mission was closed is not clear. The last resident priest left in 1822, as had many other Dominicans once Mexico became independent of Spain. El Rosario's mission continued to be served by the few remaining Dominicans from other missions. The last Dominican in the region was Tomás Mansilla, as he was traveling south in 1850.

When Mexican farmers moved into the valley, they made use of the abandoned mission tiles and other coverings for their own homes and barns. The adobe walls became exposed to rain and have slowly been eroding back to the earth. Efforts to stabilize the remaining walls with a plaster coating as well as installing gravel walkways have been made in recent years at both Rosario mission sites.

The first mission site is just off of Highway One, in the town of El Rosario. Go 0.8 mi southbound from the *Baja Cactus* motel and gas station and turn uphill for just a few hundred feet. The second mission site is across the river in the small village of El Rosario de Abajo. Turn right (west) where Highway One makes a sharp left (east) curve, just past *Baja Cactus Motel* and *Mama Espinoza's* restaurant. Then, turn left (south) at the next street in a few hundred feet and cross the river. Head west, going 1.6 miles from Highway One. The ruins are on the right (north) as you drive west through the village of El Rosario de Abajo.

Dominican Missionaries recorded at El Rosario:
Francisco Galistéo (to 1779) July 24, 1774
Miguel Hidalgo 1774 and 1780
Manuel García 1775
José Aivár 1775-1783
Manuel Pérez 1775-1788
Luis Sáles 1778
Antonio Luésma 1781-1783
Juan Antonio Formoso 1783-1788
José Estévez 1785-1787
Pedro de Acebedo 1787-1788
Pedro Gandiága 1788-1791
Miguel Abád 1789-1791
Tomás Marín 1790-1793
Jorge Coéllo 1790-1791
Ricardo Texéyro 1791-1792
Vicente Belda 1792-1798
Juan María Salgado 1794-1795
Ramón López 1797
Juan Ríbas 1797-1803
Antonio Lázaro 1799
José Caulas 1799 and 1806-1814
Segismundo Fontcubierta 1800-1801
Raymundo Escolá 1802-1807
Antonio Menéndez 1814-1815
José Jimeno Viéytez 1817
José Martín 1817-1818
José Duro 1818-1819
Francisco Troncoso 1819-1822 (last resident missionary)
Antonio Menéndez 1822-1825 (from San Vicente)
Tomás Mansilla 1829 and 1844 (from Santo Tomás)

Santo Domingo

Mission Santo Domingo circa 1880. Photo from Robert Jackson.

Mission Santo Domingo ruins in 2005. Photo by the author.

Santo Domingo mission ruins in 2017. Photo by the author.

Santo Domingo mission ruins in 2017. Photo by the author.

#20 Santo Domingo (1775-1822)

One year following the founding of their first mission at El Rosario, the Dominicans were ready to establish the second mission of their California service. Padre Manuel García and Padre Miguel Hidalgo traveled twenty *leagues* (about fifty miles) north to a site where a large arroyo emerged from the mountains. This was on or about August 30, 1775, and they named the new mission Santo Domingo. The first services were held in a cave at the base of a large red rock on the south side of the arroyo. The mission church was soon constructed near the cave.

Padre García was at Santo Domingo until late 1776, when he was succeeded by Padre José Aivár, who served until the end of 1791. Other Dominicans performed functions at Santo Domingo during his time as resident priest. One was Padre Luis Sáles, who performed baptisms here in 1778 and 1779. Sáles wrote that the Indians of Santo Domingo (and San Vicente further north) were "unquiet, subversive, and inclined to revolt." A terrible smallpox epidemic killed a third of the population in 1781.

In 1782, the mission's neophyte population was only seventy-nine. Getting Indians to live at Santo Domingo was more difficult than at other missions, where food offered by the missionaries had bribed them away from their native homes. The problem for this mission location was that most of the Indians lived along the coast or on San Quintín Bay twenty miles away and the sea provided for their subsistence. The mission's agricultural program required quantities of fresh water to grow crops and raise livestock. Fresh water was typically found in the hills but not along the seashore. Salt flats near the bay provided for the salt needs of this and the other northern Dominican missions.

The next resident missionary was Padre Miguel Abád who was stationed here from January 1792 to September 1804. In 1793, the church was constructed using adobe and poles. It measured approximately twenty-two by fifty feet. In 1798, a large chapel with additional rooms and a kitchen was constructed two and a half miles to the east, where the twenty-three-year-old mission was moved. This placed the mission closer to a better water supply.

By 1799, a cattle ranch outpost was established at San Telmo, about sixteen miles north. Construction of additional buildings continued at both Santo Domingo and San Telmo. San Telmo was an important visita of Santo Domingo and has been populated continually since mission times. By 1800, the neophyte population at Santo Domingo had increased to 315.

Padre José Miguel de Pineda was next in charge at Santo Domingo making entries in the mission books until August 24, 1809. Very few baptisms appear in the books beyond 1809 and it is uncertain if a resident priest was even living at Santo Domingo after 1821. Sea otters, sold to the Russians, were an important source of mission revenue, along with sales of salt. These activities were necessary during the period of isolation while Mexico and Spain were at war and the padres needed supplies.

Large gaps in recording events began after 1822. The next entries in the mission books were made in 1827 and 1828. The population was down to seventy-eight in 1830. The final entries made in the mission book began again in 1832 and were made each year to 1836, then again in 1838. The final baptism was on March 18, 1839.

An interesting story comes from the pen of an editor of *Desert Magazine*, the late Choral Pepper:

"In the late 1920s the buildings were still intact with embroidered altar cloths, carved wooden saints, and bells hanging from a crossbar in front of the mission. The faithful then had a superstition that so long as the bells hung in their rightful place, peace and health would dwell in the pueblo. Then one night in 1930, the bells were stolen. Immediately several older residents dropped dead. After that, the mission fell into ruin and its altarpieces disappeared.

"While editor of Desert Magazine, I was told a story by a reliable reader that might explain the disappearance of the wooden saints. On a visit to Santo Domingo, she had personally examined four carved wooden mission figures, each about three feet high and so heavy that it required the efforts of several strong men to lift them. She was told that the mission's last priest had left the saints in the care of a local farmer. Responsibility for their safekeeping had been passed from one surviving senior member of the community to the next eldest upon the death of each in turn. Originally there had been five figures, she was told, but one had been loaned to a neighboring village for a festival and never returned. At that time, they resided in a shed at the rear of a farmhouse near the mission.

"An early traveler who discovered gold dust clinging to their hollowed insides reportedly found a different set of figures, similar except in size."

To reach Santo Domingo, take a graded dirt road east for 4.6 miles from Km 169 on Highway One, just north of the Santo Domingo river crossing.

Dominican Missionaries recorded at Santo Domingo:
Manuel García (to 1776) August 30, 1775
Miguel Hidalgo 1775 and 1777-1780
José Aivár 1775-1792
Domingo Ginés 1778
Luis Sáles 1778-1779
José Díez Bustamante 1780
Manuel Pérez 1781
José Estévez 1782-1785 and 1788
Juan Antonio Formoso 1785-1787
Jórge Cóello 1789
Miguel Abád 1791-1804
Tomás Valdellón 1793-1801
Tomás Cavallero 1794
Jáime Codina 1794-1797
Miguel López 1795
Mariano Yóldi 1796
Juan Ríbas 1799
José Caulas 1799-1803
Antonio Lázaro 1800
José Miguel de Pineda 1804-1809
Manuel de Águila 1807
Ramón de Santos 1809
Bernardo Solá 1809-1811
Róque Varela 1811-1812
José Duro 1812-1819
Domingo Luna 1819-1822 (last resident missionary)
Francisco Troncoso 1821
Antonio Menéndez 1822-1825 (from San Vicente)
Félix Caballero 1822, 1827, 1829, and 1832-1834 (from San Miguel)
Tomás Mansilla 1829-1850 (from Santo Tomás)

San Vicente

San Vicente mission ruins in 1955. Photos by Howard Gulick.

Mission San Vicente, east end of church in 2017. Photo by the author.

Mission San Vicente, west end of church in 2017. Photo by the author.

#21 San Vicente Ferrer (1780-1829)

Mission San Vicente was founded on August 27, 1780, by Padre Miguel Hidalgo and Padre Joaquin Valero twenty *leagues* (about fifty miles) north of Santo Domingo. The location was well watered and at an important intersection of routes north to San Diego and east to the Colorado River.

Padre Luis Sáles became resident missionary in 1781 and was there until 1787. A violent smallpox epidemic struck San Vicente in 1781. Padre Sáles wrote that he saw many dead Indians in the fields. Sáles would look into caves only to find children nearly dead from hunger, and not of the smallpox. He and his soldiers brought the children to the mission to be returned to good health. Once the disease ran its course, life began to return to normal. In 1782, San Vicente had a native population of eighty-three and by 1787, the number had grown to 317.

A higher level of hostility by the Indians required the creation of a *presidio* (fort) at San Vicente. Padre Sáles had the mission complex enclosed by an eight-foot-high adobe wall with towers. Additionally, San Vicente had eight to ten soldiers to stand guard.

Following the Dominican strategy of expansion of the mission system, Padre Sáles made expeditions north to fill the void between San Vicente and San Diego. In 1787, Padre Sáles founded the mission of San Miguel about seventy-five miles north from San Vicente.

Padre José Estévez was in charge of San Vicente Ferrer following Padre Sáles until March 1789. Padre Miguel Gallégo then followed Estévez as resident missionary until July 1794. The church building in 1793 was an adobe structure measuring sixty feet by twenty feet; the roof was made of tules (reeds).

Padre Tomás Valdellón succeeded Padre Gallégo from October 1793 to August 1797. Padre Ramón López replaced Valdellón and made entries in the books of record until April 1806. In 1800, the population included 246 Indians. Most of the neophytes lived in their own rancherías and came to the mission on rotation for two weeks of instruction.

As at the other Dominican missions, many missionaries offered assistance to the resident padre and several Dominicans are included in the record books. Padre Pedro González made some entries in 1808. The resident Dominican at San Vicente from 1808 to 1811 was Padre José Duro, followed by Padre Antonio Fernández, who was there until November 1816. Padre Antonio Menéndez recorded two burials in 1817 and a Padre José Martínez recorded one in November 1817.

In a letter dated October 3, 1822, Padre Pineda of Santo Tomás wrote of the sad state of having so few Dominicans in Northern Baja California: "the Father of San Vicente [Antonio Menéndez] administers what is impossible, San Vicente, Santo Domingo, Rosario and San Fernando." Padre Felix Caballero was at San Vicente in 1822 and perhaps through to May 27, 1828, when the book of records was closed. Padre Tomás Mansilla was stationed at San Vicente in 1829 with an Indian population of 142. Twenty years later, the number of native Indians had dropped to seven. Most sources give the year 1833 for when the mission was abandoned.

The mission walls have been stabilized and are in a park-like setting with walkways. A staff person is sometimes available to provide commentary and tours of the mission grounds. The mission site is 0.6-mile (1 km.) west of Highway One, at Km 88.5, south of Ensenada.

A footnote: While the Dominicans were establishing their first three missions in northern Baja California, the Franciscans were also busy. In the same period of time, the Franciscans opened three missions in Alta California. This was in addition to the five they already founded in Alta California while still operating the Baja California missions between 1769 and 1773.

Dominican Missionaries recorded at San Vicente:

Miguel Hidalgo (to 1781) August 27, 1780
Joaquín Valero 1780-1783
Luis Sáles 1781-1787
José Estévez 1785-1789
Juan Antonio Formoso 1789
Miguel Gallégo 1789-1794 and 1803
José Loriénte 1790-1791 and 1794-1795
Miguel Abád 1793
Tomás Valdellón 1793-1797 and 1801-1803
Ramón López 1797-1808
Segismundo Fontcubierta 1797 and 1799
Pedro González 1808
José Duro 1808-1811
Antonio Fernández 1811-1822
Félix Caballero 1814 and 1822-1829
José Martínez 1817
Antonio Menéndez 1817-1825
Tomás Mansilla 1829 (from Santo Tomás)

Missions founded 1769-1787

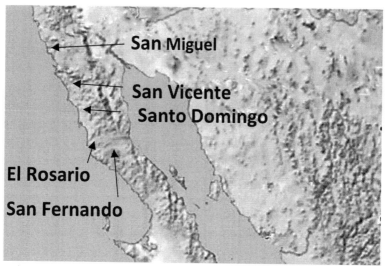

18) San Fernando, 1769
19) El Rosario, 1774
20) Santo Domingo, 1775
21) San Vicente, 1780
22) San Miguel, 1787

Christianized California Indians as illustrated by Padre Ignacio Tirsch, in service from 1762 to 1768.

Saint Junípero Serra, who was President of the California Franciscans, 1767-1784.

San Miguel ruins in 1966. Photo by Choral Pepper.

San Miguel mission ruins in 2000. Photo by Jack Swords.

San Miguel mission ruins in 2017. Photo by the author.

#22 San Miguel Arcángel (1787-1834)

The Dominicans were anxious to complete their original task to establish five missions in the void between San Fernando de Velicatá and San Diego de Alcalá. The Dominicans named this region *La Frontera*, and after thirteen years, they only established three missions. Indians hostile to the Dominican presence at San Vicente, along with the 1781 massacre at Yuma, caused a multi-year delay in beginning their fourth mission. Padre Luis Sáles of San Vicente finally explored for new sites and found one he felt suitable for the future Mission San Miguel at an arroyo named El Encino.

On March 28, 1787, Mission San Miguel Arcángel was founded midway between San Vicente and San Diego on the Camino Real. This mission site was referred to as "San Miguel Encino" or "San Miguel de la Frontera." The native population at San Miguel began with 123 baptisms the first six months and there were 137 neophytes by the end of 1787. Peveril Meigs (in 1928) reported that this first mission location at El Encino was apparently on the site of a Russian ranch named La Misión. It was located above an *encina* (oak filled canyon). Meigs was unable to locate any original mission ruins on the ranch.

Rooms and a chapel were being constructed, and crops were planted at the mission, then the spring dried up. From the writings of Padre Sáles: "While we were in this predicament there came an unbaptized Indian all swollen up from the bite of a viper and at the point of death. He was the captain (chief) of a place named San Juan Bautista. I had the good fortune to cure him perfectly with common oil [a remedy which the missionaries use regularly on such wounds]. The grateful Indian told us that in his land there were all the facilities we were seeking to found a settlement. Instantly I set out, explored the site, and found that what the Indian had said to me was true. Consequently, we abandoned this place and moved all the train to the new site ..."

This new site (San Juan Bautista) was just over seven miles west of El Encino (the first mission site) and one-and-a-half miles from the coast. An estuary and the beach near there provided abundant seafood. The area was also well populated with Indians. The San Miguel mission was moved to San Juan Bautista in 1788. The Indian name for the area was *Ja-kwatl-jap*, (ja=water; kwatl=a family name; jap=hot) for some warm springs in the valley. A source for salt was nearby at La Salina, along the coast, adding even more value to an area that seemed like a perfect location for growing crops and raising livestock.

That same year, Padre Sáles incorporated into San Miguel a ranchería of Indians located in Franciscan territory, midway between the two missions of San Miguel and San Diego. The Governor approved Sáles' request to moving the boundary line with the Franciscan jurisdiction fourteen miles north from the Médano Valley to Rosarito Creek (*Arroyo del Rosarito*). It remained the division between Baja and Alta California until the end of the Mexican War, when it was moved north again to the Tijuana River Valley.

In 1793 the adobe church measured nineteen feet by seventy-two feet and was roofed with tiles. Inside were two altars. The missionaries also had an adobe dwelling. In 1794 the population numbers were up to 206. An irrigation canal was built along the steep slope, next to the mission. The canal ran from over a kilometer away. In 1798, three rooms and two granaries were built. In 1800, a new house for the missionaries and their servants was built. That same year 224 Indians were converted at San Miguel. However, a few years later, in an 1808 report, Dominican Presidente Ramón López said this: "Conditions at San Miguel are not very good. While outwardly prosperous, its minister can barely provide the Presidente with twenty-five or thirty pesos annually. I know quite well that the priest there can hardly meet his own needs."

Normal instructions and orders from Spain, as well as supplies from the Mexican mainland, were interrupted and the missionaries and Spanish soldiers had to fend for themselves for some eleven years of isolation during the war for Mexico's independence, beginning in 1810. The Dominicans appealed to their Franciscan brothers in Alta California for assistance in 1815. The Alta California missions were doing far better and were able to respond with cattle, grain, and clothing. Large fields had been cultivated at San Miguel but flash floods carried off most of the soil by 1810.

The damage from these floods was so severe that in 1810 Padre Tomás de Ahumada had moved the mission about eight miles north to a place named El Descanso. The new site was known also as "San Miguel la Nueva" (New San Miguel). Padre Ahumada traveled between the two sites while based at Descanso but seems to have eventually returned mission functions to the old site. In 1824, the estimated population was 350-400. However, in 1830 the population was only seventy-eight.

Following the 1821 independence of Mexico from Spain, the original purpose of the missions to convert the Indians into civilized Spanish subjects was over. The padres, however, continued to serve the native Indians. In 1830, Padre Félix Caballero had new adobe buildings erected at El Descanso, reviving activities there. While El Descanso is not technically a separate mission from San Miguel, it is considered such by Mexico's National Institute of Anthropology and History (INAH) and most history writings. See page 171.

No mission activities are recorded beyond 1834 at ether San Miguel or El Descanso. On December 29, 1840, the Dominican President, Padre Gabriel González, asked Padre Tomás Mansilla of Mission Santo Tomás to include the missions of San Miguel and Guadalupe in his jurisdiction. This indicates that the Dominican leadership either did not know of or ignored the abandonment of those two missions.

The new Mexican government secularized mission property throughout Mexico in 1833, but the remoteness of California (Baja and Alta) and the number of Indians who were not yet "civilized" or transformed into "European style" living caused an exception in the law to be added in 1835. A California mission could continue to operate until the current missionary died or until he abandoned it.

The 1788 San Miguel mission site is located next to Highway One (the Ensenada "Free Road") in the modern town of La Misión, Km. 65.5, twenty-seven miles north of Ensenada.

Dominican Missionaries recorded at San Miguel:
Luis Sáles (to 1789) March 28, 1787
Caietano Pallás 1790-1791
Juan Salgado 1792-1793
Mariano Yóldi 1793-1804
Mariano Apolinário 1794-1796
Raymundo Escolá 1797-1800
Miguel Abád 1799
Tomás de Ahumada 1809-1815
Félix Caballero 1815-1834
José Martínez 1819-1822 (last resident missionary)
Domingo Luna 1829 and 1833

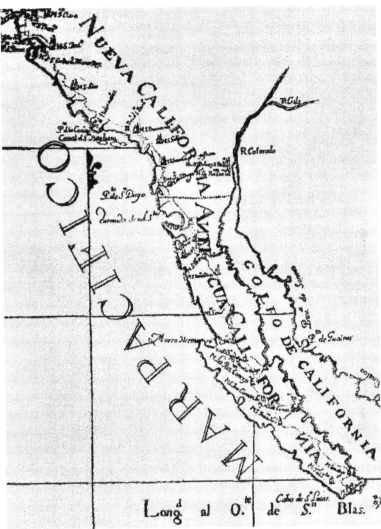

The 1787 map by Padre Francisco Palóu shows the California missions, El Camino Real, and the division line between Franciscan Nueva (New) California and Dominican Antigua (Old) California.

1791 Site for Santo Tomás

Santo Tomás first site ruins in 1975. Photo by Robert Jackson.

Santo Tomás first site remains in 2005. Photo by the author.

1794 Site for Santo Tomás

Santo Tomás second site in 1998. Photo by Kevin Clough.

Santo Tomás second site in 2009. Photo by the author.

1799 Site for Santo Tomás

Santo Tomás third site in 1926. Photo by George Hendry.

Santo Tomás third site in a 2017 photo by the author.

#23 Santo Tomás de Aquino (1791-1849)

The location for the twenty-third Baja California mission was discovered in 1769 and named San Francisco Solano by Franciscan Padre Juan Crespí. In April 1785, "San Solano" was visited by Dominican Padre Luis Sáles and a party of soldiers from the mission of San Vicente while searching for potential mission sites. On one of the Padre Sáles expeditions to San Solano, he was attacked by the native Indians, wounded, and thrown from his horse. Sáles, "half-dead," hid while the Indians chased the soldiers, who returned later to rescue the Dominican priest.

Mission Santo Tomás de Aquino was founded by Padre José Loriénte on April 24, 1791 in the San Solano Valley. This was at a place called by the natives *Copaitl Coajocuc* (crooked sycamore). With this mission established, the Dominicans fulfilled their mandate to occupy the frontier territory between Mission San Fernando de Velicatá and San Diego. The wide gap along El Camino Real between San Vicente and San Miguel was bridged. The Indian neophyte population in the first year at Santo Tomás was ninety-six.

A 1793 report described the mission church as a small adobe structure fourteen feet by thirty-four feet with a roof of poles and mats. A dwelling for the missionaries was also constructed of the same materials. This first location chosen for the mission had been questioned by Governor Fages because it could be swept away by floods being in the narrow part of the canyon. Also, sunlight would be blocked a third of the day by the height of the hills.

According to a missionary's letter, sickness developed the second year at Santo Tomás and he attributed the problem to the marsh: "The heathen did not live where the mission is, but further up the plain, where the air is pure and there are no mosquitoes or gnats because the land is clearer."

As the result of continual problems of mosquito infested swamps and general unhealthy conditions at the first site, on May 31, 1794, the mission was moved a mile east and higher up the valley. This placed it on the north side of the arroyo, with full sunlight. A new church building was made of adobe with a roof of poles and tules (reeds). Another building of the same materials was made for the priests.

Horses, mules, cattle, sheep, and goats were all raised at the mission. Grain was planted and yields increased, yet in 1798 Padre Miguel López wrote to the governor asking that the mission be moved one more time further east, where more land could be put under cultivation.

In 1799, the mission did relocate again. The final move made was just over three miles to the east, where four buildings were constructed. In 1800, work continued on the church and other buildings. The neophyte population reached the highest at 262. The church was eighty-five feet long and eighteen feet wide with a flat, earth-covered roof. A sacristy was constructed twenty feet by fifteen feet in size. Several other buildings were erected before 1801, including storerooms and living quarters for single girls.

Raising crops and livestock all were successful at the third site for the mission. Trading with foreign sea captains at the bay of Ensenada (Ensenada de Todos Santos) twenty miles to the north was reported. This exchange was an important source of revenue during years of isolation while Mexico was fighting Spain for independence from 1810 to 1821.

In the same year, two Dominican priests while serving at Santo Tomás were murdered by mission Indians. Miguel López was killed on January 13, 1803 at the hands of an

Indian by the name of Mariano Carillo. Eudaldo Surroca was killed on May 17, 1803. Surroca was found dead in his bed, the body was full of bruises and bone fractures. At least three Indian domestics were involved, one confessed immediately to the crime. Of the three, one was a woman named Barbara Gandiága who instigated the killing of not only Surroca but of López, four months earlier.

The year was 1849 and while Padre Tomás Mansilla was visiting Mission San Diego de Alcalá he left his brother, Agustín Mansilla y Gamboa, in charge at Santo Tomás. On June 10, 1849, Agustín wrote to his brother Tomás that people traveling north for the gold fields were stealing from locals and from the church. An Indian was reported to have stolen altar valuables and sold them to the "Forty-niners" passing through. That seemed to be the final straw. Tomás Mansilla returned from San Diego, abandoned his mission, and traveled south to join Padre Gabriel González in the southernmost region of Baja California. Mission Santo Tomás de Aquino was the last operating California mission, closing in 1849.

None of the three sites for this mission have any kind of preservation. They are all on private property and INAH has not performed any kind of protection as of this writing. The photos illustrate the inevitable vanishing of these unprotected adobe buildings.

The first (1791) site is nearly gone, with just a small section of wall remaining next to an oak tree picnic area, along a running stream. From Highway One on the north side of the Santo Tomás Valley, take the graded dirt road west (signed for La Bocana and Puerto Santo Tomás). Go 3.4 mi and take a road to the left and go a half mile more to the clearing next to the picnic area. In 2017, this former picnic area was closed.

The second (1794) mission site had only a small area of melted adobe and rocks and was in a planted field when visited in 2009. It was a few hundred feet north of the same La Bocana road, about a mile closer to Highway One than the first site. The distance from Highway One to the second site is 2.8 mi. In 2012, satellite imaging showed the adobe area of the mission having been removed and planted over. Confirmed in 2017. Another mission site gone!

The 1799 third and final site is on the east side of Highway One at the town of Santo Tomás. As you enter Santo Tomás from the north, look near the tall palm trees just north of the El Palomar campground. The mission aqueduct is near the site and still carries water from the spring.

Some books mention only two sites for Santo Tomás. Some books have called the second site "the first," never mentioning the extensive adobe complex once seen at the true first site. Some books have not mentioned the second site, mentioning only the first and final site. Some have reported that road construction destroyed one site. I have found adobe remains at all three sites that match locations photographed in the past ninety years and identified as mission sites.

Photographs show how the unprotected adobe brick walls are susceptible to weathering. In a 1916 letter, about his 1887 expedition to save Dominican artifacts, Fr. James Newall, O.P., made the following very poignant remark:

"But let us say at once, we found very little to describe. Since Mexico's achievement of independence from Spain, and the expulsion of the Spanish Friars from the Peninsula -- that is, for a period of seventy years -- those missions had been utterly abandoned, and, what is worse, adventurers and interlopers from Sonora -- who constitute the present owners of the Mission lands -- after driving and killing off the Indians, dismantled the churches and monasteries, seized on and sold the valuable church furniture and works of art, and even tore the tiles from the Mission roofs for their own huts, thus exposing the walls to the dissolving action of the rains, so that there is hardly a Mission in that country of which it might not be said, *Etiam ruinae perierunt! Even the ruins have perished."*

Dominican Missionaries recorded at Santo Tomás:
José Loriénte (to 1798) April 24, 1791
Miguel López 1793-1803
Segismundo Fontcubierta 1798
Eudaldo Surroca 1802-1803
Juan Ríbas 1806
José Miguel de Pineda 1812-1826
Tomás Mansilla 1826-1849

California Indian men, women, and infants illustrated by Padre Miguel Venegas in 1739 (published in 1757 as *Noticia de California*). Note the baby in a carrier-net.

The Final Three Spanish Missions

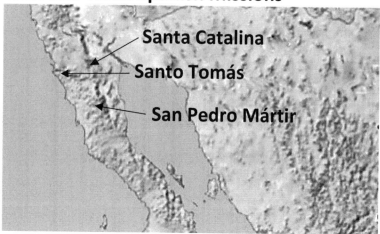

23) Santo Tomás, 1791
24) San Pedro Mártir, 1794
25) Santa Catalina, 1797

San Pedro Mártir ruins in 2004. Photo by Jack Swords.

#24 San Pedro Mártir de Verona (1794-1811)

By the end of 1791, the first five Dominican California missions were established along El Camino Real, securing and defining the corridor between the peninsular missions and San Diego. The interior could now be brought under Dominican influence with "mountain missions." The Indian attacks would be halted by "Christianizing the heathens," or so the Spanish government believed.

The northern Baja California mountain valleys and meadows were first explored by a Spanish soldier named José Velázquez in November 1775. Velázquez was ordered by Governor Neve to explore the northern gulf coast for a port closer than the Bay of San Luis Gonzaga to serve the new Dominican missions. Velázquez traveled north from Mission San Fernando found many Indians as well as oak and pine forests, crossing west to east over what would become known as the Sierra San Pedro Mártir. He climbed a high peak and saw the Colorado River and the surrounding desert but never left the sierra due to the uncertainty of finding drinking water. Velázquez was of the opinion that the Colorado River, where they would reach it, would be mostly sea water, thus not drinkable. Even though the goal of the expedition was not met, Velázquez did spark a desire of the Dominicans to establish a mission in the higher elevations of Baja California. In April 1785, Velázquez and California Governor Pedro Fages explored east from Mission San Vicente to the Colorado River seeking land routes from Mexico to California. Hostile Indians they encountered along the river would end further expeditions for over a decade.

In May 1793, California's Lieutenant Governor José Joaquín de Arrillaga, in Loreto, authorized an expedition to find potential mountain mission sites. Two sites were found to be the most suitable. One was northeast of San Vicente near a pass (El Portezuelo) leading to the Colorado River. The other potential mission site was east of Mission Santo Domingo in a high mountain meadow. In a letter dated January 15, 1794, Arrillaga stated that Mission San Pedro Mártir would be founded east of Santo Domingo that April.

Mission San Pedro Mártir de Verona was established on April 27, 1794, by Padre Caietano Pallás with Padre Juan Pablo Grijálva and Padre José Loriénte. The first site for the mission was at a place known to the native Kiliwa Indians as *Casilepe* and is a meadow, today called La Grulla. It was at an elevation of 6,785 feet. The exact location was unknown to historians until an expedition in 1991 revealed cut-stone foundation blocks in a pattern and scale that was of European origin. Some sixty Kilawa Indians joined the mission in its beginning.

Less than three months passed from its founding before a location change was requested. On July 18, 1794, Padre Pallás wrote the following to Governor Borica: "The new foundation has not continued with the happiness with which it began. The crops have frozen and I have determined to move it to work at another place, situated on the western slope of the Sierra about three leagues distant from the other." On July 19, 1794, Padre Pallás wrote: "The missionary at San Pedro Mártir says he will move the week that now ends, because of frosts and annoyances." On July 29, Pallás requested permission to execute the transfer from Casilepe to the location that was known to the Kilawa natives as *Ajantequedo*. Governor Borica responded on August 10 to permit the transfer to a more fertile and sheltered site. The second mission site is seven miles south but more importantly it is over 1,700 feet lower in elevation than the first.

The mission was in a region where the Kiliwa Indians only visited seasonally. A large workforce was not easy to assemble without there being a permanent local population. The complex at *Ajantequedo* was large and mapped out by Peveril Meigs during his field work on the Dominican missions in 1926. It resembled a fort with defensive walls for protection. Water for mission crops came from springs on opposite sides of the valley and above the stream. Irrigation canals were built from the two springs and both ran for a half mile to the fields and to the mission. In 1926, Meigs found the mission floors were partly tiled with red nine inch square bricks, and pieces of red roof tiles were abundant. Meigs stated that San Pedro Mártir was a "highly developed, picturesque, and unique mission." The elevation at the second site is 5,060 feet above sea level, making it the highest Spanish California mission.

In 1794 Sergeant José Manuel Ruiz wrote of the building of two *bulwarks* (fortifications) with cannon *embrasures* (openings). Ensign Alférez Bernal had been sent from San Vicente to San Pedro Mártir in May 1796 to investigate an incident; Bernal found that some soldiers were wounded and some Indians killed in a skirmish. Lieutenant Governor Arrillaga left Loreto by boat in June 1796 for Bahía San Luis Gonzaga then traveled by land to Mission San Vicente. Arrillaga wrote in August 1796 that there was additional trouble with Indians "escaping." While at San Vicente, Arrillaga learned that the neophytes of San Pedro Mártir had deserted and demanded that a new padre be assigned to them.

By 1800, the population had grown to only ninety-two. The primary crop was corn, but raising cattle was the most productive endeavor for this mission thanks to the extensive nearby pasturelands. In 1801, a new church made of adobe seventeen feet by sixty-nine feet and a long reception room thirty-nine feet by nineteen feet were constructed. Also, two rooms each nineteen feet by twenty-two feet plus a storage room nineteen feet by thirty-three feet were built. Sometime after 1801, the mission fell into decline. The lack of surviving records makes the cause for decline open to speculation.

In 1808, Padre Ramón López wrote a report on the status of all the peninsula missions. In it he states, "The two missions in the hills, Santa Catalina and San Pedro [Mártir], cannot give what they don't have. The minister at Santa Catalina formerly was able to send something, but now he struggles just to make ends meet. San Pedro [Mártir] is good for little more and likely will always be that way." From this report, we learn that the mission existed at least until 1808. Once the mission was abandoned the remaining neophytes were transferred to Mission Santo Domingo. Details are uncertain about the cause for the abandonment or the exact year it closed. One research paper states that an especially cold winter closed the mission in 1811 (see also page 216).

The San Pedro Mártir mountain range is named for the mission. This mission is one of only two in Baja California not accessible by automobile. A two or three-day backpack or mule ride is required to reach the site. The usual approach is from San Isidoro, a mission visita ruin, then steeply up the mountain on the mission trail. See photo on page 216. These articles give additional details about this mission:

John Robertson, 1966 (page 39):
http://dezertmagazine.com/mine/1966DM08/index.html

John Foster, 1991:
http://www.pcas.org/Vol33n3/333fostr.pdf

Max Kurillo, 1996:
http://www.pcas.org/Vol33N3/333Krilo.pdf

Dominican Missionaries recorded at San Pedro Mártir:
Caietano Pallás, Pablo Grijálva, and José Loriénte Apr. 27, 1794
Rafaél Caballero 1794-1797
Antonio Caballero 1794-1797
Juan Ríbas 1797
Mariano Apolinário 1797-1798
José Caulas 1798
Miguel López 1798
José Loriénte 1798
Eudaldo Surroca 1803
José Portela 1806
Juan Ríbas 1806
Ramón de Santos 1806

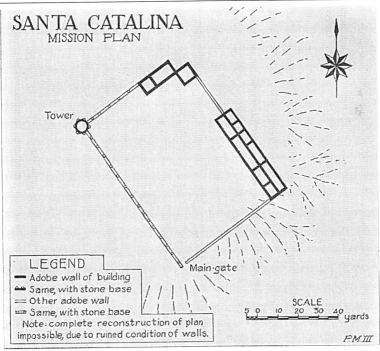

1926 plan of Mission Santa Catalina site by Peveril Meigs.

Mission wall foundation corner. Photo by Lee Panich in 2007.

Santa Catalina mission ruins in 2018. Outlines of the mission rooms along the northeast side of the complex. Photo by the author.

#25 Santa Catalina Virgen y Mártir (1797-1839)

The Mission Santa Catalina story begins with the actions of Padre Juan Crisóstomo Gómez while serving as Dominican President from 1790 to 1793. Gómez authorized three mountain missions founded to secure the inland areas of the northern peninsula and to Christianize the natives. Immediately after the founding of the first mountain mission of San Pedro Mártir, the search for the second mission site began in the region as directed by the viceroy.

In October 1794, Sergeant José Manuel Ruiz and Padre Tomás Valdellón examined the place named Santa Catalina midway between the mission of San Vicente and the Colorado River. The most important aspect of a mission site was a reliable year-round source of water that was present at Santa Catalina. A year later, Ensign Alférez Bernal led an expedition in exploration of the same region. Governor Borica provided Bernal with a list of "prime essentials" a mission site must possess. The list included a constant source of water, land for raising wheat and maize, nearby firewood and pasture, and numerous available "heathen."

Lieutenant Governor José Joaquín de Arrillaga, traveled north from his home in Loreto. He left Mission San Vicente on September 5, 1796, to examine Santa Catalina and the route to the Colorado River. This was but one of four expeditions that year to determine if a land route to Sonora was feasible. Arrillaga had met hostile Indians at the Colorado River and returned to San Vicente by way of San Diego.

Arrillaga had desired to separate California into two political districts, and his 1796 expedition was to be influential in that happening. Governor Borica also favored the plan, yet nothing came of it for several more years.

163

In an October 1797 letter, Arrillaga determined that a garrison of soldiers should be stationed in the delta region with a presidio at the head of the gulf and a detachment at Sonoita and San Felipe, thus securing a sea route of escape. The first order of business, however, was to establish a mission at Santa Catalina.

The order for a new mission was placed by the viceroy and the governor. The mission was to be strongly fortified as it was known to be in dangerous territory. Santa Catalina would also be the last mission built on the peninsula authorized by the Spanish government. No other potential mission site was so greatly researched by repeated expeditions than Santa Catalina.

On August 6, 1797, building was begun at the future mission site for the church (measuring thirty-three feet by seventeen feet), a priest's house (seventeen feet square), and a guardhouse. November 12, 1797, was the day that Mission Santa Catalina Virgen y Mártir was officially founded by Padres José Loriénte and Tomás Valdellón. It was the seventh Dominican California mission, as well as the twenty-fifth mission founded on the peninsula. The location was called by the natives *Jaca-Tobojol*, which means "place where the water falls over stones." The elevation at Santa Catalina is 3,900 feet above sea level.

In 1798, an adobe house with two rooms was built with each room measuring fourteen feet by seventeen feet. In 1799, another adobe house measuring fourteen feet by twenty feet was constructed to serve as a shelter for girls and single women.

Santa Catalina had a population of 133 Indians in 1800. Another house measuring seventeen feet by seventeen feet was also built that year. In 1802, an adobe structure with two rooms measuring fourteen feet square was constructed and may have served as a workshop.

Governor Borica died in July 1800, shortly after leaving Alta California for Durango. Arrillaga was made governor but was allowed to remain at his residence in Loreto rather than move to Monterey. In four years, Arrillaga would finally achieve his desire for two Californias.

California was officially divided into two districts on March 26, 1804. Arrillaga was made governor of Alta California, and Captain Felipe de Goycoechea was appointed governor of Baja California. The line that separated the two Californias was the same as that established by Padre Luis Sáles in 1788, at Arroyo del Rosarito. It had separated Dominican founded Mission San Miguel Indians from those belonging to Franciscan Mission San Diego to the north.

The original plan for a third mountain mission, as ordered by Padre Gómez, was abandoned. The reason was mentioned previously in the San Pedro Mártir chapter; a letter was written in Loreto on December 23, 1808 by the Dominican Padre Ramón López. López wrote of the declining conditions at the two mountain missions: "The two missions in the hills, Santa Catalina and San Pedro [Mártir], cannot give what they don't have. The minister at Santa Catalina formerly was able to send something, but now he struggles just to make ends meet."

The population at Santa Catalina was reported as more than 600 in 1824, dropping to 250 by 1834. This would have made Santa Catalina the most populous of the Dominican founded missions, according to the reports made.

In October 1839, the Santa Catalina mission was attacked burned, and sixteen neophytes were slain. Neither Padre Caballero, nor any other Dominican ever returned to rebuild Santa Catalina.

The walls have melted back into the ground, leaving almost nothing to visualize the once important mission. Archeologists in recent years have excavated to the stone foundation at a corner of a mission room and have accurately mapped the site with sophisticated equipment. The Pai-pai Indians are still living near the mission. Their village is called Santa Catarina, which is a slightly different spelling than the mission's name.

To reach the Santa Catalina mission site next to Santa Catarina, use the Ensenada-San Felipe highway (Mexico Three) and drive just south of Km 91, in the town of Ejido de los Heroes de la Independencia. Go east, on a concrete-paved road. 4.7 miles from Highway Three, the road becomes unpaved. Go downhill, then work left through the little town of Santa Catarina, soon going over a hill to the cemetery. Turn left and go up the hill, above the cemetery. The mission site is 5.5 miles from Highway Three.

Dominican Missionaries recorded at Santa Catalina:
José Loriénte (to 1798) November 12, 1797
Tomás Valdellón 1797-1804
Jacinto Fiol 1804-1807
Manuel de Aguila 1807-1809
Antonio Fernández 1809-1810 and 1815-1817 (from San Vicente)
José Duro 1810-1811
Manuel Saiz 1811-1812
Félix Caballero 1819-1839

The End of Spanish Control

Mexico and Spain were at war from 1810 to 1821. In 1822, the two Californias pledged their allegiance to Mexico. The Spanish mission era was over, but the need for religious instruction and expanding civilization necessitated the missions to remain in operation. Two additional missions would be added. Many Dominicans retired from service in Baja California in 1822. The last Dominican who came to Baja California to serve the missions was José de Santa Cruz in 1841. The last Dominican missionaries on the peninsula were Tomás Mansilla and Gabriel Gonzáles, who left Baja California together from La Paz on or about February 5, 1855.

Those Dominican missionaries that remained after 1822, or arrived during the Mexican mission period include:

Félix Caballero (to 1840)
Gabriel Gonzáles (to 1855)
Domingo Luna (to 1832)
Tomás Mansilla (to 1855)
José Martínez (to 1836)
Juan Martínez (to 1840)
Antonio Menéndez (to 1825)
José Morquecho (to 1841)
José Miguel de Pineda (to 1826)
Ignacio Ramírez (to 1849)
José de Santa Cruz (to 1844)

Assisting the Dominicans in Baja California were three priests of the Mercedarian Order, who arrived in 1836:

Amado Aldana (to 1841)
Vicente Sotomayor (to 1851)
Ascenscio Torres (to 1845)

The Last Missions

26) El Descanso 1810 and 1830 sites
27) Guadalupe (del Norte) 1834

The 1830 Descanso mission, in 1927. 'Fort' is the 1810 ruin location. Photo by Peveril Meigs.

The 1810 Descanso site ruins. Photos by Jack Swords.

The 1830 Descanso mission ruins. Photos by Jack Swords.

#26 El Descanso (1810-1834)

The history of El Descanso is told without the usual documentation available for most missions. From the few notes and letters that have survived, we know that Padre Tomás de Ahumada arrived at his new post at Mission San Miguel in mid-1809. Not long after his arrival, a flood devastated the mission's fields. By 1810, Ahumada had relocated the mission to El Descanso, eight miles north.

Perhaps the biggest question is if El Descanso is truly a separate mission at all or just an alternate location for San Miguel. The El Descanso site was often called "San Miguel la Nueva" (New San Miguel) by the Dominicans. The earlier San Miguel was afterward called "Misión Vieja" (Old Mission). Both locations were served by only one priest, and Spanish government officials had no input on this action by Ahumada. While El Descanso is perhaps not technically a separate mission from San Miguel, it is considered such by Mexico's INAH and many history writers.

The following letter by Padre Ahumada (resident missionary of San Miguel between June 1809 and February 1815) provides the evidence for when mission activities were moved to El Descanso. The letter was written from San Miguel, indicating Ahumada had returned there. It is possible he operated both locations simultaneously as a mission and visita.

"This mission [San Miguel] lost its irrigable lands in some floods, when I had just recently come to it, and I moved the mission to Descanso, which is eight [sic] leagues to the north where there are some moist lands. This ground was located beside the Arroyo del Mogano, where wheat and barley are grown by dry farming with some abundance. I discovered a valley which I named Santo Domingo, where there is more than sufficient land for any kind of cultivation at any time of the year. A beautiful lagoon provides the moisture throughout the whole year, offering abundant soil suitable for growing corn and beans. There are a church and living quarters for all seasons of the year.

"In San Marcos (to the east of San Miguel) one can direct at small cost a river of water which descends a nearby sierra and is lost in a sandy arroyo. It is the one that brought the above-mentioned flood to the ruined mission."

Ruins of Padre Ahumada's Descanso mission may be those now at a cemetery, overlooking the Descanso valley from the south rim. Peveril Meigs (in 1927) identified the location as a "fort" since it commands a strategic location. It somewhat mirrors the placement of the San Miguel mission, which also is above and overlooking a valley from the south side.

Padre Felix Caballero was the next Dominican assigned to San Miguel, starting in May 1815. Caballero would remain in charge in northern Baja California for the next twenty-four years. By 1819, Caballero was also serving the needs of Mission Santa Catalina. Padre José Martínez was also at San Miguel from 1819 to 1822, and it is unknown how much time (if any) was spent at El Descanso. Unknown is the year Padre Caballero moved primary mission operations from Descanso back to San Miguel or if both locations had equal status as one mission at two sites.

What is clear is that Padre Caballero reestablished El Descanso in 1830 with the construction of new buildings. Caballero employed the Indians of the tribe of Chief Jatiñil for the new construction. Caballero's mission is in the valley, on the north side of the arroyo, opposite the older ruins. Three and a half miles up the valley from El Descanso was a mission orchard of some twenty acres. A twenty-five-foot square reservoir next to a spring and a 500-yard long irrigation ditch were documented in 1927 by Peveril Meigs at this site. It is named La Viña after a huge grapevine there.

In June 1834, Caballero moved mission functions from both El Descanso and San Miguel to his new church of Nuestra Señora de Guadalupe, about fifteen miles east of San Miguel.

In 1879, Manuel Clemente Rojo produced historical notes on activities in Baja California to replace documents destroyed during an 1843 rebellion in La Paz. One of these notes contains an interview with Chief Jatiñil of the mountain Indians that states Jatiñil has been the chief since 1822. His father and grandfather were chiefs before him because command of the tribe has always been in the hands of his family, and that is why the tribe bears his name. He continued with: "I helped Father Caballero build Mission El Descanso from its foundation to the end." Jatiñil also helped Caballero build Mission Guadalupe in 1834 but would later turn against the Dominican padre because the Jatiñil people were being forcibly baptized.

The El Descanso mission walls had all eroded away by the 1950s and a new church was constructed on the site. Many locals were not even aware of its existence in the 1960s, according to history writer Choral Pepper who labeled Descanso as a "lost mission." Foundation ruins were exposed in a 1997 archeological dig, and then the site was partially covered by a steel awning.

The 1830 ruins are next to a modern church and are partially protected by the awning. Use the free Ensenada highway, Mexico One, to Km 49 and take the dirt road going east, under the toll highway to the church, 0.5 mile. This is just south of the Cantamar sand dunes.

While El Descanso functioned as a mission, there is little doubt that it was originally only a new location for Mission San Miguel. The name, El Descanso (Place of Rest), was the location and was not a saint's name as all missions had used. In reality, this was "New San Miguel," at El Descanso. However, the church constructed in 1830 might be considered the first Mexican mission in Baja California.

The boundary between the Dominican administration and Franciscan administration of California was first marked by Franciscan Padre Palóu in 1773 at the next valley just north of El Descanso, Arroyo el Médano. In 1788, the line was moved further north by Padre Luis Sáles to Arroyo del Rosarito.

Dominican Missionaries recorded at El Descanso:
Tomás de Ahumada 1809-1815
Félix Caballero 1815-1834

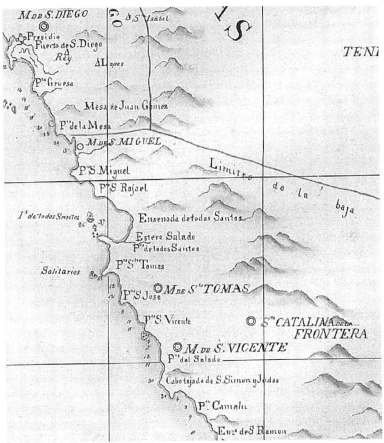

Map from 1823 showing the missions of San Vicente, Santa Catalina, Santo Tomás, San Miguel, and San Diego. Notice no Mission El Descanso is shown as it wasn't a separate, unique mission, at least until 1830.

Photos of foundation ruins at Guadalupe mission site in 2012. Photos by the author.

#27 Nuestra Señora de Guadalupe (1834-1840)

Ojá Coñúrr (Painted Rock) was the native Indian name for the location of the final mission to be established in both Baja and Alta California. Dominican Padre Félix Caballero named this new mission in honor of Mexico's patron saint, Guadalupe. The founding date has been given as June 25, 1834. The mission is sometimes called "Guadalupe del Norte" to differentiate it from the Jesuit Mission Guadalupe (1720-1795) in southern Baja California.

Padre Caballero arrived in northern Baja California in late 1814. The records show he performed a burial service at Mission San Vicente on December 15 of that year. In May 1815, Caballero was assigned to Mission San Miguel to replace Padre Tomás Ahumada, who had been the resident missionary there since 1809. Caballero was one of just five missionaries in northern Baja California that year.

In 1819, two more Dominicans arrived in Baja California and Felix Caballero was placed in charge of Mission Santa Catalina from 1819 to 1822. Major events transpired in 1822 for the people of Baja California. They learned that Spain had lost Mexico after eleven years of war and they were to pledge their allegiance to the new Mexican Empire. Also in 1822, Chilean ships and soldiers, led by English Admiral Thomas Cochrane, attacked San José del Cabo, Todos Santos, and Loreto in an attempted invasion.

Mexico's new emperor, Agustín de Iturbide, was soon banished by General Santa Anna, and the young country became a republic. The California missions would continue to operate without any government assistance, as they had done for several years during the war. The few remaining mission padres had to survive on what they could raise or from trading goods with foreigners. Padre Caballero was able to succeed at Mission El Descanso, which he re-founded in 1830. Some potentially rich farmlands were just southeast in a valley called San Marcos. Caballero was anxious to develop the valley. Chief Jatiñil, who helped Caballero build the new church at El Descanso, also helped him construct this new mission. Jatiñil came from Nejí, in the mountains, twenty-five miles northeast.

Guadalupe, like the new church at El Descanso, was a personal project of Caballero. The Spanish mission program was over, and while Mexico ordered that the missions be secularized in 1833, the law was rescinded for the California missions in 1835. They could continue to operate and serve the Indians until each mission was abandoned or the priest of that mission died.

According to the research of Rev. Albert Nieser, O.P., Caballero built the mission for newly arriving mainland settlers, not the Indians. Chief Jatiñil provided help for Caballero every year with harvesting crops as well as constructing Caballero's mission buildings. Jatiñil also helped Caballero in fighting other Indian tribes that attacked Mission Santa Catalina. Jatiñil's father had told him that the land would belong to the *gente de razon* or "people of reason" (whites and mixed bloods), and the chief had accepted this reality.

The Guadalupe mission church had two altars and a choir loft. The mission compound had shops and a residence for the priest. Caballero made Guadalupe the administrative center of the northern peninsula missions. The mission sat on a small mesa overlooking the valley from near the center-west side. Two miles of irrigation canals were constructed down both sides of the valley. One six-acre plot, just north of the mission, was where vegetables and fruit were raised. Cattle seemed to be the chief commodity with nearly 4,915 head reported in 1840, the largest of any Dominican mission. A letter to Caballero on May 29 of that year from Don Juan de Jesús Ozio, however, claims the count was only 1,915.

In 1836, some 400 Yuma Indians attacked Guadalupe but the garrison of soldiers stationed there were able to save the mission. More attacks came until the final one by Caballero's own supporter, Chief Jatiñil. He revolted against Caballero because the priest continued to force baptism of his tribe and tried to make them live at the mission. An attack in October 1839 was reported to have sacked the mission, but an eye-witness to the attack gave the date as February 1840, as recorded by Manuel Clemente Rojo. Jatiñil's goal was to kill Padre Caballero, but the padre was able to persuade María Gracia, an Indian woman, to hide him in the mission's choir loft. Caballero escaped death and left northern Baja California for Mission San Ignacio in the southern half of the peninsula. There he began to acquire property and attempted to have his Guadalupe mission cattle delivered to him.

On the morning of August 3, 1840, at Mission San Ignacio, Caballero said Mass and drank his daily cup of chocolate. Sharp stomach pains hit him, as though he had been poisoned. Felix Caballero died a few hours later. The extensive property of Caballero would cause government officials in Baja California to frown on the Dominicans who remained. The missions were in decline, the Indians were few in number, and the mission churches often continued to serve the newly arriving mainlanders. Dominicans were replaced by parish priests. The last operating California mission to close was Santo Tomás in 1849. The last two Dominicans left Baja California from La Paz in 1855. Catholic parish priests had been replacing the Dominican missionaries at several of the old missions during those final years.

By 1929 the adobe walls of Mission Guadalupe were already destroyed by treasure hunters, but some of the wall's stone foundation was present and measured sixty yards on one angle and thirty yards on the other. Pieces of red floor tiles were inside the angle. It was reported that broad steps led down the slope from the mission to two cement water tanks fed by a spring.

In recent years, the mission site has been developed as a historical park and includes a museum. It is located in Francisco Zarco (the government's official name for the town of Guadalupe). Take the paved side road going into town from the gas station on Highway Three. In about a mile, turn left at the cross street (where the road ahead becomes divided). The mission and museum are overlooking the river valley.

Dominican Missionaries recorded at Guadalupe (del Norte):
Félix Caballero 1834-1840

Epidemics

The biggest failure of the California mission system was the unintentional introduction of diseases from Europe and the mainland of Mexico that the native California population had no resistance to. By the time there was an understanding of how to reduce the rate of infection and even inoculate against it, the damage was done and the native population could not recover. Smallpox was the first and biggest killer followed by measles which killed many in later years. Another major cause of population reduction was from syphilis, introduced by Spanish soldiers. Syphilis attacked women of child-bearing age and children in the womb were most vulnerable. Poor pre-natal care of infants suffering dehydration led to many infant deaths. This was blamed on the end of traditional tribal or family instruction that existed before the missionaries changed the native living habits. Abortion became common and possibly provoked by the stress of poor mission living conditions during the later Franciscan and Dominican period. Dr. Robert Jackson goes into great detail in his 1994, *Indian Population Decline, The Missions of Northwestern New Spain, 1687-1840.*

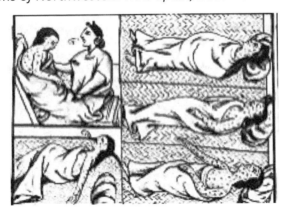

The stages of smallpox, introduced by Spaniards, and death of Native Americans. Illustrated in *The Florentine Codex*, 1577.

After the Missions Closed

Many of the missions fell into ruin after the last missionary left his station. A few, well-built adobe or stone structures remained intact or were maintained and continued to serve as parish churches with a new priest or one who visited from another location.

Santo Domingo, San Borja, Santa Gertrudis, San Ignacio, Mulegé, La Purísima, Comondú, Loreto, San Javier, San Luis Gonzaga, Todos Santos and San José del Cabo continued as local religious centers, after the Dominicans left.

Santo Domingo, La Purísima, Comondú, Loreto and San José del Cabo churches fell into ruin or were demolished in the early 1900s. Today, nothing survives of the original mission churches of La Purísima, Comondú (except a preserved side chapel), and San José del Cabo. The Loreto mission church had no roof or bell tower prior to reconstruction in the 1950s.

Other locations may have some walls, graves, or foundations or just rubble or mounds of what once were adobe bricks since melted by the rain or damaged by treasure hunters. Todos Santos has had post-mission construction added to the older walls. Two have newer churches built on top of the former mission buildings (Santiago and San José del Cabo) and a couple have nothing left to see from the original construction other than modern markers (Ligüí and La Paz).

San Borja, Santa Gertrudis, San Ignacio, Mulegé, San Javier and San Luis Gonzaga are the best examples of original mission church construction standing intact, today. The walls of the Loreto church and the side chapel at Comondú are also examples of Jesuit-era construction.

Relocated Baja California Missions

Nearly half of the missions were moved one or more times following their founding. Often a mission would be called by the new location name rather than the original, official name. Sometimes the official name was changed with the move; all of this has naturally caused some confusion over the years. The common mission name is used for the missions in this book except in the headings for each mission chapter.

Listed below are the thirteen missions that relocated, how often, and the greatest distance moved from the founding location:

San Javier, 1 time, 5 miles south
Comondú, 1-2 times, 24 miles south
La Purísima, possibly 1 time, 10 miles south*
La Paz/Todos Santos, 2 times, 50 miles south
Los Dolores/La Pasión, 1-2 times, 16 miles southwest
Santiago (Aiñiní), 1 time, 2 miles south
San José del Cabo, 3 times, 5 miles north
Calamajué/Santa María, 1 time, 23 miles northwest
El Rosario, 1 time, 2 miles west
Santo Domingo, 1 time, 3 miles east
San Miguel, 3 times, 8 miles north
Santo Tomás, 2 times, 4 miles east
San Pedro Mártir, 1 time, 7 miles south

*Details of the move are inconclusive. Foundation ruins do exist at a possible first site, now called Purísima Vieja.

Missions that Never Were and Lost Missions

One thing Baja California literature is not lacking in is the number of missions referred to that never were missions or were mythical, secret, or "lost missions."

Travel in Baja California before the mid-1970s involved hundreds of miles of unpaved and often challenging roads. The adventure of the trip itself inspired many to write books about their excursion. Even before automobiles, when mules and burros were the means of travel, the peninsula inspired writers to share the adventure in print. Some of the more notable "mission" stories are documented below, whether the stories are disproved or not, the imagination and searching will no doubt continue.

Santa María Magdalena

One of Baja California's first adventure books was Arthur North's *Camp and Camino in Lower California*. North traveled the peninsula in 1905 and 1906 and his book was published in 1910. The missions and *El Camino Real* (The Royal Road or King's Highway) were the focus of his expedition. North's historical details were not always accurate, and many writers in the following years repeated his errors in their own books.

One of Arthur North's errors was presuming that the La Magdalena ruins, seventeen miles northwest of Mulegé, were the proposed Jesuit mission of Santa María Magdalena. The Santa María Magdalena mission project was planned for the region far north of San Ignacio, as shown on the 1757 Jesuit map.

Books and maps published after North's would continue to call the Magdalena site near Mulegé "Mission Santa María Magdalena." No documentation supports this site as ever having been that or any other mission.

In 1966, mystery novel author Erle Stanley Gardner and his associates in off-road vehicles discovered some strange walls, thirty-five miles south of Bahía de los Ángeles that baffled explanation. On that expedition was *Desert Magazine* editor Choral Pepper, who later researched Jesuit writings and maps and concluded that the Gardner expedition had indeed found the "true" Santa María Magdalena site, 140 miles from North's Magdalena. Perhaps this was an abandoned mission project after all? One of the bells hanging at the nearest mission to the south (Santa Gertrudis) reads "Santa María Magdalena 1739." Was the bell intended for the mission that never was?

The mission of San Luis Gonzaga had a visita also named Santa María Magdalena (on the large bay of the same name). It was planned to be developed into a mission according to the Report of 1744. There is no other connection between the two sites.

To continue progress in California and obtain funding, the Jesuits listed their missions in a 1745 report. In that report are three northern, unfinished missions, which are also shown as "started" on their 1757 map. Santa María Magdalena, Dolores del Norte, and San Juan Bautista are these three missions.

This mysterious wall was found by Choral Pepper and others exploring uncharted regions in central Baja California. Her research later concluded this was the unfinished mission project shown on the 1757 Jesuit map and named Santa María Magdalena. The location was forgotten by those on that expedition thirty-five years later when interviewed by the author. Finding this "lost mission" was a quest of the author and a great personal reward after several years searching for it. Additional photos: http://vivabaja.com/109

Dolores del Norte

Another Erle Stanley Gardner "lost mission" presumed to have been discovered was Dolores del Norte. Using helicopters to explore and locate rock art sites north of San Ignacio, back in the early 1960s, Gardner and friends came upon the small village of San Francisco de la Sierra. It was so remote that it had no automobile road and the expedition members brought in by helicopter were the first "outsiders" anyone in the village had ever seen. When *Desert Magazine* editor Choral Pepper asked villagers the significance of the old stone walls, they answered "Dolores." While the mountain people may have really believed the walls were part of a mission named Dolores, the Jesuits' documents do shed the light of truth on this mystery. Dolores del Norte was to be the next mission north of San Ignacio. When funding and a new missionary was finally available to open the mission, the name was changed to Santa Gertrudis, to honor the wife of its benefactor.

The adobe mission visita ruins in San Pablo Canyon, between San Ignacio and Santa Gertrudis, have also been called "Mission Dolores del Norte" by INAH. Some maps also show a mission of that name in the desert south of El Arco. In reality, the name Dolores del Norte existed only on paper and the mission of Santa Gertrudis is what became of it.

San Juan Bautista (Santa Clara)

The third mission the Jesuits listed on their 1745 report and the 1757 map as 'started,' was named San Juan Bautista. The 1757 map has it located west of San Ignacio in the Sierra Santa Clara, north of Punta Abreojos. While there is at least one reliable water spring in these desert hills, no ruins have ever been documented to exist. The Lost Santa Clara Mission legend is well-known to locals.

When the Jesuits were expelled from the New World by order of King Carlos III, some believe they had advance warning and collected all their valuable church possessions and treasures to hide in a secret mission. Santa Clara is considered by many as the best choice for this mission.

A Californian, with his catch of rats, as illustrated by Padre Jakob Baegert. Published four years after his mission service (1751-1768).

1757 Jesuit Map showing missions as they existed about ten years earlier. Three missions in the north (San Juan Bautista, Dolores del Norte, Santa María Magdalena) are shown on this map as "started." Only Dolores del Norte was actually established with the name changed to Santa Gertrudis.

Santa Isabel

The most well-known Baja California lost mission legend is that of Santa Isabel. Unlike San Juan Bautista, not one word is mentioned of a Mission Santa Isabel on maps or documents from the Jesuits. Only a single water source along the gulf coast by that name is shown on their map. It is located between San Felipe and Bahía San Luis Gonzaga. This has led many lost mission hunters to explore the desert hills north of the last known Jesuit mission of Santa María.

The Santa Isabel legend developed out of suspicions about the Jesuits activities in California. They controlled the peninsula as an independent theocracy with full control of who came and left. Stories of accumulated treasures secreted away by the padres in one last, hidden mission were born and make entertaining reading. The truth is that the missions were always on the edge of economic failure. If not for the supplies from the mainland and generous benefactors in Europe, the missions in Baja California would have never survived.

Perhaps searching for lost missions in Baja California is more of an excuse or a reason to do some desert exploring. This author has enjoyed hiking with others seeking "lost missions," knowing full well no treasures ever existed. The missionaries suffered great poverty, and the challenges to stay alive occupied most of their efforts, leaving no time available to collect treasures!

Others

Often books or maps have shown *visitas* as being missions or sometimes a mission's second location as being a unique mission. Some sites that were never missions but shown as missions on maps include San Juan Londó, San Miguel (de Comondú), La Presentación, and El Novillo.

Calamajué is often shown or listed as either a mission or a visita. The documents clearly show that Calamajué was the first location for the seventeenth Jesuit mission. In less than a year, that mission was moved and renamed "Santa María."

Near the modern town of Los Barriles (south of La Paz) a 1721 mission of Ensenada de las Palmas is sometimes shown or mentioned. This was simply an early proposed location for what would become Mission Santiago, established further inland. The first Santiago mission was begun in 1722 and known as Santiago de los Coras. However, that project was abandoned the following year when the church wall collapsed and killed many of the Cora Indians. In 1724, the mission was again started, but further south in the land of the Pericú Indians.

The Jesuits had made two earlier attempts to gain a foothold in California before the founding of the Mother Mission at Loreto. The first was in 1683 at La Paz and was called Guadalupe. The second was begun a few months later at San Bruno, fifteen miles north of Loreto. This colony was abandoned in 1685. These two colony attempts did provide the Jesuit, Padre Kino, with insight of how to succeed in California and that led to the success of Loreto in 1697.

One visita of Loreto was named Nuestra Señora de los Dolores and listed as a mission by Padre Píccolo in his *Informe* (report) of 1702. This should not be confused with the 1721 founded mission of Dolores, seventy miles south from Loreto. The 1721 mission was often called "Dolores del Sur" by the Jesuits in order to prevent confusion with the older visita.

Afterword

The missions of Baja California are historically significant, intriguing, and colorful as to their existence. That such great effort was made in such extreme conditions illustrates the commitment and steadfast faith the missionaries had for their work in peninsular California. The native Indians who survived mixed with the mainlanders and foreigners who came to the peninsula. The Indian tribes in the north were better able to survive the changes and live today in villages on the Colorado River Delta, near Mission Santa Catalina, and near Mission Guadalupe.

The history and details of the mission period in Baja California continue to enlighten and entertain us with stories about this harsh and rugged land so many years ago. Much more can and should be written as the stories of the missions are far from over. This author welcomes new historical discoveries that can and should be made in this fascinating land that was: *The First California.*

Loreto, the mother mission of both Lower and Upper California. How it may have appeared in the late 1700s or early 1800s. Illustration by Rivera Cambas in *A History of Lower California*, 1960.

Appendix A: Chronology

The following are significant events in the history of Baja California's missions.

1534 Spanish sailors led by Fortún Jimenez are the first Europeans to arrive in California at La Paz.

1535 Hernán Cortés establishes a colony at La Paz, it fails in two years.

1539 Francisco de Ulloa sails the entire coast of the Gulf of California and part way up the Pacific Coast, proving California is a peninsula, not an island.

1540 As part of the expedition by Francisco Vázquez de Coronado, Hernado de Alarcón sails to the Colorado River Delta. Melchior Díaz travels there by land and is the first Spaniard to cross the Colorado River into California.

1542 Juan Rodríguez Cabrillo sails the entire Pacific Coast of Baja California and beyond to San Diego and the Channel Islands.

1596 Sebastián Vizcaíno establishes a colony at Cabo San Lucas. It fails in just two months.

1602 Sebastián Vizcaíno sails the Pacific Coast of California and renames the places previously named by Cabrillo.

1683 Padre Eusebio Francisco Kino and others attempt to establish a mission in California, first at La Paz then at San Bruno. The project fails after two years.

1697 Padre Juan María de Salvatierra establishes the first permanent mission and colony in California, at Conchó, and names the mission Loreto.

1699 The second mission, San Francisco Javier, is founded by Padre Francisco María Píccolo.

1701   Padre Salvatierra crosses the gulf to join Padre Kino to seek a land route to California and they travel within sight of the Colorado River Delta to confirm this. A mission at Guaymas, Sonora was founded to support the California missions.

1705   The next missions, at Ligüí and Mulegé, are founded.

1708   San José de Comondú is the fifth mission founded.

1720   California's first ship *El Triunfo de la Cruz* is built using güéribo trees found west of Mulegé; La Purísima, Pilar de la Paz, and Guadalupe missions are founded.

1721   Padre Juan de Ugarte sailed from Loreto north to the Colorado River Delta to again prove California was not an island; Mission at Ligüí is abandoned and a new, mission called Los Dolores is established further south at Apaté; Padre Ignacio María Nápoli explores for a new mission south of La Paz.

1722   Nápoli builds Mission Santiago de los Coras, at Santa Ana, but tragedy forces its abandonment.

1724   Mission Santiago el Apóstol is founded, at Aiñiní.

1728   Mission San Ignacio is founded in the north and remains an important frontier mission for many years.

1730   Mission San José del Cabo founded as the southernmost California mission.

1733   Mission Santa Rosa de las Palmas is established at the La Paz mission visita of Todos Santos.

1734   The Pericú Indian uprising begins; two Jesuits and many others are killed. All four of the southernmost missions are attacked. They are abandoned by Spanish personal for two years.

1737   Mission San Luis Gonzaga is founded.

1746 Padre Fernando Consag sails to the Colorado River Delta, again proving California is not an island. Jesuits now want to build missions around the Gulf of California. Consag later leads two land expeditions seeking mission sites north of San Ignacio.

1748 Mission Pilar de la Paz is moved south to Todos Santos and replaces Mission Santa Rosa there. San José del Cabo mission is reduced to a visita of Santiago.

1752 Mission Santa Gertrudis is founded as the first mission north from San Ignacio.

1762 Mission San Borja is founded as the next mission northbound.

1766 An expedition led by Padre Wenceslaus Linck of San Borja discovers Velicatá as a potential new mission to the north. The seventeenth and last Jesuit mission is founded midway to Velicatá, at Calamajué. It is relocated in less than a year and renamed Santa María de los Ángeles.

1767 Orders for the expulsion of the Jesuits by King Carlos III arrive in California at San José del Cabo on November 30, but are not revealed until December 26, at Loreto.

1768 All sixteen Jesuits are removed from California and replaced two months later by the Franciscan missionaries led by Padre Junípero Serra. San José del Cabo regains mission status. The two missions of San Luis Gonzaga and Los Dolores are closed by José de Gálvez. The neophytes of both missions are relocated to Todos Santos.

1769   Junípero Serra leads the overland expedition to San Diego with new orders to occupy Alta California, which is what the land north of the peninsula is called. Serra founds the first Franciscan California mission at Velicatá and names it San Fernando.

1773   A division marker separating Alta and Baja California was placed at Médano Valley by Padre Francisco Palóu. Dominican missionaries assume control of all Baja California missions.

1774   The first Dominican founded mission is opened and named El Rosario.

1775   The next mission is founded and named Santo Domingo. Mission Santa María is abandoned.

1780   Mission San Vicente Ferrer is founded.

1787   Mission San Miguel is founded.

1788   Division line between Franciscan Alta California and Dominican Baja California is moved fourteen miles north to Arroyo del Rosarito by Padre Luis Sáles, with government approval.

1791   Mission Santo Tomás is founded.

1794   Mission San Pedro Mártir is founded.

1795   Missions Guadalupe and Santiago are abandoned.

1797   Mission Santa Catalina is founded.

1804   California is officially divided into two political regions of Spain (Baja California and Alta California).

1809   Soon after arriving at Mission San Miguel, floods there cause Padre Ahumada to move the mission to El Descanso. Later he returns to the former site.

1810   Mexico declares its independence from Spain. In the ensuing war mission supplies become restricted.

1811   Mission San Pedro Mártir is abandoned.

1817   Mission San Javier is abandoned.

1818   Mission San Borja is abandoned.

1822   Both Californias pledge their loyalty to the new Mexican Empire; Chile attempts an invasion of Baja California with the help of English Admiral Thomas Cochrane. They attack several missions; Missions Santa Gertrudis, San Fernando, and El Rosario are abandoned when many Spanish Dominicans return to Europe.

1824   Mexico becomes a republic.

1826   Mission La Purísima is abandoned.

1827   Mission San José de Comondú is abandoned.

1828   Mission Santa Rosalía de Mulegé is abandoned.

1829   A storm closes the mission of Loreto and the capital of Baja California is moved to La Paz. Mission San Vicente is abandoned.

1830   Padre Felix Caballero builds a new church at El Descanso and calls it a mission.

1833   Mexico orders all missions to be secularized. Mission lands begin to be sold off by government officials in Alta California.

1834   Padre Felix Caballero establishes the last mission in the Californias and names it Guadalupe; San Miguel and El Descanso missions are abandoned.

1835   The California missions get an exemption from the secularization decree as missionaries convince officials the native Indians are still in need of the missions.

1839   Attacks by Indians at the missions of Santa Catalina and Guadalupe. Both are soon forced to close.

1840   Nearly all remaining open missions cease operations, although some continue as parish churches.

1846 War between Mexico and the United States begins. U.S. forces soon occupy Baja California. Two years later during peace negotiations, Baja California is returned to Mexico. The border line is moved fourteen miles north from Arroyo del Rosarito.

1849 The last California mission in operation closes at Santo Tomás.

1855 The last Dominican missionaries in Baja California leave from La Paz.

Mission San Borja in 2013. The northernmost stone mission church in Baja California was constructed during the Dominican period. Photo by Chris Glass.

Appendix B: Jesuits in California (1683-1768)

The sixty Jesuits are listed here with the year they arrived in California followed by the year they left or died in California including the missions where they served. Some variation exists in the spelling and years among the reference sources.

Lucas Alvarez* 1742
Juan Armésto 1747-1753: Loreto
Vicoriano Arnés 1764-1768: San Borja, Santa María

Francisco Badillo 1752-1762: Santiago
Jakob Baegert 1751-1768: San Luis Gonzaga
Johann Balthasar* 1745-1746
Miguel Barco 1737-1768: San José del Cabo, San Javier
Juan Basaldúa 1702-1709: San Javier, Mulegé
Johann Bischoff 1746-1768: San Luis Gonzaga, Santa Rosa, Loreto, La Purísima, Todos Santos
Jaime Bravo 1705-1744: Loreto, Pilar de la Paz

Lorenzo Carranco 1726-1734: Santa Rosa, Santiago
Fernando Consag 1733-1759: San Ignacio
Jean Baptiste Copart 1683-1685**

Juan Díez 1765-1768: San Borja, Calamajué, La Purísima
Jacobo Druet 1732-1753: La Purísima
Benno Ducrue 1750-1768: La Purísima, Guadalupe

José Echeverría* 1729-1730
Francisco Escalante 1757-1768: Mulegé, Santiago

Francisco Franco 1764-1768: Todos Santos, Loreto

Andrés García* 1737
Joseph Gasteiger 1735-1754: Guadalupe
Matías Goñi 1683-1685**
William Gordon 1728-1738: La Paz, Mulegé, San Javier
Clemente Guillén 1714-1748: Ligüí, Loreto, Dolores

Everard Hellen 1720-1735: Guadalupe
Lambert Hostell 1737-1768: San Luis Gonzaga, San José del Cabo, Dolores

Franz Inama 1750-1768: Comondú

Eusebio Kino 1683-1685**

Wenceslaus Linck 1762-1768: San Borja
Ignacio Lizazoáin*1761-1762
Francisco López 1755-1764: Loreto
Agustín Luyando 1730-1738: San Javier
Juan Luyando 1727-1734: San Ignacio, Mulegé

Julián Mayorga 1707-1736: Loreto, Comondú
Jerónimo Minutili 1702-1703: Loreto
Juan Mugazábal 1704-1761: Loreto

Ignacio Nápoli 1721-1726, 1736: Santiago
Pedro Nascimbén 1735-1754: Mulegé
Karl Neumayer 1746-1764: Santiago, San José del Cabo, Todos Santos

Francisco Osorio 1725-1727: La Purísima

Francisco Peralta 1709-1711: Ligüí
Francisco Píccolo 1697-1729: Loreto, San Javier, Mulegé

Georg Retz 1751-1768: Santa Gertrudis
José Rondero 1745-1751: Comondú
José Rotea 1758-1768: San Ignacio

Julián Salazar 1758-1765: Loreto, Mulegé, Santiago
Juan Salvatierra 1697-1717: Loreto
Sebastián Sistiaga 1718-1747: Mulegé, San Ignacio

Nicolás Tamaral 1717-1734: Mulegé, San Javier, La Purísima, San José del Cabo
Sigismundo Taraval 1730-1750: La Purísima, San Ignacio, Santa Rosa, San José del Cabo, Santiago
Antonio Tempis 1736-1746: Santiago
Ignacio Tirsch 1762-1768: Loreto, Santiago
Gaspar Trujillo 1744-1748: Loreto, San José del Cabo
Joaquín Trujillo 1755-1757: Mulegé

Juan de Ugarte 1700-1730: Loreto, San Javier
Pedro de Ugarte 1704-1707: Loreto, Ligüí

Lucas Ventura 1757-1768: Loreto
Juan Villavieja 1765-1768: Loreto

Franz Wagner 1737-1744: Comondú

Bernhard Zumziel 1737-1751: La Paz, Santa Rosa

* Visitador General only, not a resident priest in Baja California.
** Original Colony Attempt of 1683 at La Paz and San Bruno

Appendix C: Franciscans in Baja California

The first Franciscans to replace the Jesuits arrived near Cabo San Lucas on December 2, 1767. They reached Loreto on March 12, 1768 only to learn that they would be going back across the gulf once their brother Franciscans, led by Junípero Serra, arrived. Padre Serra and the other sixteen Franciscans would occupy the missions after their arrival at Loreto on April 1, 1768.

The Franciscans were administrators of the peninsula missions for five years. This list shows the Franciscans at each of the sixteen missions they operated with the first year of their service at the named mission(s). Los Dolores and San Luis Gonzaga missions were both abandoned during the Franciscan administration.

Gregorio Amurrio 1771 Santa Gertrudis
Pedro Arriguibar 1771 Mulegé

Dionisio Basterra* 1768 Santa Gertrudis
Juan de Medina Beitia* 1768 Santa María, 1769 San Ignacio

Miguél de la Campa y Cos* 1768 San Ignacio, 1769 San Fernando, Santa María
Juan Crespi* 1768 La Purísima

Francisco Eschasco 1771 La Purísima
Juan Escudero 1769-1771 San Javier

Juan Figuer 1771 San Borja, Todos Santos
Vicente Fuster 1771 San Fernando, Santa María

Juan Ignacio Gaston* 1768 Mulegé, 1769 La Purísima
Francisco Gómez* 1768 Dolores

Vicente Imas 1771 San José de Comondú

Manuel Lago 1771 Guadalupe
Francisco de Lasuén* 1768 San Borja, 1769 Santa María
José Legomera 1771 San Ignacio
Antonio Linares 1771 San Fernando, Santa María

Antonio Martínez* 1768 San José de Comondú, 1769 La Purísima
Juan Moran* 1768 San José del Cabo
José Murguía* 1768 Santiago, 1769 Todos Santos, 1770 Loreto

Martín Palacios 1771 La Purísima
Francisco Palóu* 1768 San Javier
Fernando Parron* 1768 Loreto, San Javier
Tomás de la Peña 1771 San José de Comondú
Juan Prestamero 1771 San José de Comondú

Juan Ramos de Lora* 1768 Todos Santos, 1769 Loreto
Juan Antonio Riobó 1771 Santiago, 1771 San José del Cabo

Miguel Sánchez 1771 Todos Santos
Vicente Santa María 1771 Loreto
Juan Sancho de la Torre* 1768 Guadalupe, 1770 Santa Gertrudis
Marcelino Senra 1771 Todos Santos
Junípero Serra* 1768 Loreto, 1769 San Fernando
Benito Sierra 1769 Mulegé

Ramón Uson 1771 San Javier

Andrés Villaumbrales* 1768 San Luis Gonzaga, 1769 San Borja, 1770 Guadalupe

Francisco Villuendas 1771 San José del Cabo, Santiago

*Members of the group of sixteen Franciscans assigned to the missions on April 5, 1768.

Ruins of Visita San Juan de Dios in 2000. Photo by the author. In 2006, a farmer plowed-over and destroyed the historic site. Some of the ruins were unearthed to view in 2017.

Appendix D: Dominicans in Baja California

Listed alphabetically are approximately 100 Dominicans in Baja California with service years and associated missions. Names not followed with missions or years indicate missing data:

Miguel Abád 1789 San Fernando, 1789-1791 El Rosario, 1791-1804 Santo Domingo, 1793 San Vicente, 1799 San Miguel

Pedro de Acebedo 1787-1788 El Rosario, 1788-1789 San Fernando, 1795 Loreto

Manuel de Aguila 1804-1806 San Fernando, 1807 Santo Domingo, 1807-1809 Santa Catalina

Tomás de Ahumada 1805-1809 San Borja, 1809-1815 San Miguel, 1815 San Fernando, 1815-1821 Mulegé

José Aivár 1773-1776 San Borja

Mariano Apolinário 1794-1796 San Miguel, 1795 San Fernando, 1797-1798 San Pedro Mártir

José Armésto 1773 Todos Santos, 1790 Loreto

Rafaél Arviña 1792-1795 Guadalupe, 1795-1796 San José del Cabo, 1796-1797 Mulegé, 1796-1799 San Fernando, 1799-1802 San Ignacio, 1802-1804 Loreto, 1804-1805 San Ignacio

Vicente Belda 1792-1798 El Rosario, 1797-1798 San Fernando, 1798-1802 Loreto, 1802-1805 Mulegé

Antonio Berraguerro 1793 Loreto

José Díez Bustamante 1773-1777 Santa Gertrudis, 1778 San Fernando, 1780 Santo Domingo

Antonio Caballero 1792-1794 San Borja, 1794-1797 San Pedro Mártir

Félix Caballero 1814 and 1822-1829 San Vicente, 1815-1834 San Miguel, 1819-1839 Santa Catalina, 1822, 1827, 1829 and 1832-1834 Santo Domingo, 1840 San Ignacio

Rafaél Caballero 1792-1794 San Borja, 1794-1797 San Pedro Mártir

Joaquín Cálvo 1794-1795 San Ignacio

José Caulas 1797-1798 San Fernando, 1798 San Pedro Mártir, 1799-1803 Santo Domingo, 1799 and 1806-1814 El Rosario

Tomás Cavallero 1794 Santo Domingo

Jaime Codina 1794-1797 Santo Domingo, 1798 San Fernando

Jorge Coéllo 1789 Santo Domingo, 1790-1791 El Rosario, 1790-1795 San Fernando, 1797-1798 San José de Comondú

Antonio Concepción

Romantino de la Cruz 1812 San Javier

José de Santa Cruz 1841-1844 San José del Cabo

José Duro 1807-1808 San Fernando, 1808-1811 San Vicente, 1810-1811 Santa Catalina, 1812-1819 Santo Domingo, 1818-1819 El Rosario, 1822 Todos Santos

Raymundo Escolá 1797-1800 San Miguel, 1802-1807 El Rosario

José Espín 1794-1798 Santa Gertrudis, 1805 San Ignacio,

José Estévez 1773-1775 Santiago, 1775-1782 La Purísima, 1782-1785 and 1788 Santo Domingo, 1785-1787 El Rosario, 1785-1789 San Vicente, 1790-1791 San José de Comondú

Antonio Fernández 1809-1810 Santa Catalina, 1811-1822 San Vicente

Mariano Fernández 1790-1811 Todos Santos

Vicente Fernández

Jacinto Fiol 1804-1807 Santa Catalina

Segismundo Foncubierta 1797 and 1799 San Vicente, 1798 Santo Tomás, 1800-1801 El Rosario, 1800 and 1802 San Fernando, 1812 Santa Gertrudis

Juan Antonio Formoso 1773 La Purísima, 1783 Santa Gertrudis, 1783-1788 El Rosario, 1785-1787 Santo Domingo, 1785-1788 San Fernando, 1789 San Vicente

Francisco Galistéo 1773 La Purísima, 1773-1774 San Fernando, 1774-1779 El Rosario, 1779-1789 Loreto
Miguel Gallégo 1789-1794 and 1803 San Vicente, 1794 San Javier, 1795-1798 Mulegé, 1795 and 1810 Loreto
Pedro Gandiága 1773-1774 Santa María, 1773-1790 San Fernando, 1788-1791 El Rosario
José García
Manuel García 1773-1775 San Borja, 1775 San Fernando, 1775 El Rosario, 1775-1776 Santo Domingo, 1776-1780 Santiago
Domingo Ginés 1773 San Javier, 1778 Santo Domingo
Juan Crisóstomo Gómez 1773 San Ignacio
José María Góngora
Gabriel Gonzáles 1825-1840 Todos Santos, 1846-1848 San José del Cabo, 1850-1855 Todos Santos
Pedro González 1804 San Fernando, 1808 San Vicente
Pedro Juan González 1806 and 1812-1822 San Ignacio
Pablo Grijálva 1794 San Pedro Mártir

José Herrera 1783-1794 Mulegé, 1793-1794 Loreto
Miguel Hidalgo 1773-1774 Santa María, 1773-1777 San Fernando, 1774 and 1780 El Rosario, 1775 and 1777-1780 Santo Domingo, 1780-1781 San Vicente, 1781 Loreto
Francisco Hontiyuélo 1790-1794 Santiago, 1794 San José del Cabo

José Lafuente 1773 San José del Cabo
Antonio Lázaro 1797-1798 San Borja, 1799 El Rosario, 1799-1804 San Fernando, 1800 Santo Domingo, 1802 San Borja, 1806 Loreto
Miguel López 1793-1803 Santo Tomás, 1795 Santo Domingo
Ramón López 1797 El Rosario, 1797-1806 San Vicente, 1798 San Pedro Mártir, 1812-1816 Loreto
José Loriénte 1790-1791 San Vicente, 1791-1798 Santo Tomás, 1794-1795 San Vicente, 1794 and 1798 San Pedro Mártir, 1796 San Ignacio, 1797-1798 Santa Catalina
Antonio Luésma 1773 Mulegé, 1781-1783 El Rosario, 1782-1783 San Fernando
Domingo Luna 1819-1822 Santo Domingo, 1822-1826 La Purísima, 1829 and 1833 San Miguel

Tomás Mansilla 1825-1826 San José de Comondú, 1826-1849 Santo Tomás, 1829 El Rosario, 1829-1850 Santo Domingo, 1829 San Vicente, 1844 El Rosario
Tomás Marín 1789 San Fernando, 1790-1793 El Rosario
José Martín 1812-1816 San Borja, 1816-1818 San Fernando, 1817-1818 El Rosario
José Martínez 1817 San Vicente, 1819-1822 San Miguel
Antonio Menéndez 1814-1815 El Rosario, 1815 and 1822-1825 San Fernando, 1817-1825 San Vicente, 1822-1825 Santo Domingo, 1822-1825 El Rosario
Vicente Mora 1773-1800 Loreto
Nicolás Muñóz 1773 Guadalupe, 1779 Loreto

José Naranjo 1783 Mulegé

Caietano Pallás 1790-1791 San Miguel, 1794 San Pedro Mártir, 1794-1798 Loreto
Bonifácio Gómez de la Peña

Manuel Pérez 1773-1794 San Javier, 1775-1788 El Rosario, 1775, 1778, 1780, and 1782 San Fernando, 1781 Santo Domingo

José Miguel de Pineda 1804-1809 Santo Domingo, 1812-1826 Santo Tomás

Mélchor Pons 1794, 1797-1798, and 1803 San Borja

José Portela 1804 San Fernando, 1806 San Pedro Mártir, 1812 Mulegé

Ignacio Ramírez 1835-1841 San José del Cabo

Juan Ríbas 1797-1803 El Rosario, 1797 San Pedro Mártir, 1799 Santo Domingo, 1806 Santo Tomás, 1806 San Pedro Mártir

Manuel Rodríguez 1773 Santa Gertrudis

José Manuel Rúiz

Manuel Saiz 1811-1812 Santa Catalina

Antonio Salas 1773 Santiago

José Fernández Salcedo 1773 Todos Santos

Luis Sáles 1773-1778 Guadalupe, 1778 El Rosario, 1778-1779 Santo Domingo, 1778-1781 San Borja, 1781-1787 San Vicente, 1787-1789 San Miguel

Juan María Salgado 1792-1793 San Miguel, 1794-1795 El Rosario, 1795-1796 San Borja

José Antonio Sánchez 1793-1822 La Purísima, 1812 San José de Comondú

José de Santa Cruz 1841-1844 San José del Cabo

José Santolárria 1773 Guadalupe

Ramón de Santos 1806 San Pedro Mártir, 1808-1813 San Fernando, 1809 Santo Domingo, 1812 San Borja

Plácido Sanz 1798 Loreto, 1803-1810 San José de Comondú, 1804 Loreto

Bernardo Solá 1809-1811 Santo Domingo, 1811-1814 San Fernando

Gerónimo Soldevilla 1773 San José del Cabo, 1784-1810 San Javier
Andrés Souto 1773 San José de Comondú
Eudaldo Surroca 1797-1798 San José del Cabo, 1802-1803 Santo Tomás, 1803 San Pedro Mártir

Ricardo Texéyro 1791-1792 El Rosario, 1794-1796 San José de Comondú
Domingo Timón 1795-1798 San Ignacio, 1798-1800 Mulegé
Jacinto Tiól 1812-1820 Todos Santos
Francisco Troncoso 1819-1822 El Rosario, 1819-1822 San Fernando, 1821 Santo Domingo

Tomás Valdellón 1793-1801 Santo Domingo, 1793-1797 and 1801-1803 San Vicente, 1797-1804 Santa Catalina
Joaquín Valero 1773-1800 Mulegé, 1780-1783 San Vicente, 1783 Guadalupe, 1788 Santa Gertrudis
Róque Varela 1811-1812 Santo Domingo
Cristóbal de Vera 1773 San José de Comondú
José Vidaurréta
José Jimeno Viéytez 1817 El Rosario
José García Villatoro 1773 San Ignacio

Mariano Yóldi 1791-1792 San Javier, 1793-1804 San Miguel, 1796 Santo Domingo

Pablo María de Zárate 1796 Loreto, 1798-1821 San José del Cabo
Martín Zavaleta 1773 Loreto, 1783 La Purísima, 1793 San Borja

Appendix E: The Mission Benefactors

The Pious Fund for California was established to build and operate the California missions. In addition to the specific mission sponsors listed here, others including religious groups donated to the California cause. A pledge of 10,000 pesos was needed to sponsor a new mission, but the actual cost was much higher.

Loreto: Juan Caballero y Ocio
San Javier: Juan Caballero y Ocio
San Juan Bautista (Ligüí): Juan Bautista López
Santa Rosalía de Mulegé: Nicolás de Arteaga
San José de Comondú: José de la Puente Peña (also known as the Marqués de Villapuente)
La Purísima: José de la Puente Peña
Pilar de la Paz: José de la Puente Peña
Guadalupe: José de la Puente Peña
Los Dolores: José de la Puente Peña
Santiago: José de la Puente Peña
San Ignacio: Padre Juan Bautista de Luyando
San José del Cabo: José de la Puente Peña
Santa Rosa: María Rosa de la Peña (Marquesa de las Torres)
San Luis Gonzaga: Luis de Velasco
Santa Gertrudis: José de la Puente Peña
San Borja: María de Borja (Duquesa de Gandia)
Calamajué/Santa María: María de Borja
      The Donations:
Juan Caballero y Ocio 44,000 pesos for two missions.
Juan Bautista López Bankrupt, funding lost for one mission.
Nicolás de Arteaga 12,000 pesos for one mission.
José de la Puente Peña (Marqués de Villapuente) 167,540 pesos for eight missions.

Juan Bautista de Luyando 10,000 pesos for one mission.
María Rosa de la Peña (Marquesa de las Torres) 10,000 pesos for one mission.
Luis de Velasco 10,000 pesos for one mission.
María de Borja (Duquesa de Gandia) 62,000 pesos for two missions.

Northern portion of the 1747 map made by Fernando Consag, S.J., missionary at San Ignacio (1733-1759) following his sea expedition of 1746.

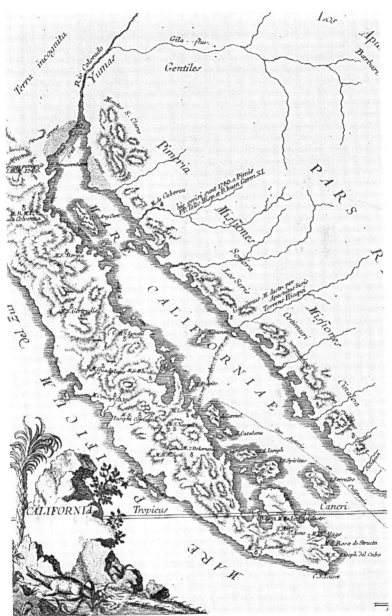

1772 Map of California from Jakob Baegert, S.J., missionary at San Luis Gonzaga (1751-1768). The 1766 founded mission at Calamajué is included and here named Nuestra Señora de Columna.

Locating Mission Sites in Baja California

GPS directions will assist in finding the mission related sites on Internet satellite maps or while traveling in Baja California. Some sites are vanished or nearly vanished and others have large stone churches that can be seen from some distance. Most are reached on dirt roads which can change or be damaged by storms but typically can be traveled to in any vehicle. A few may be reached easier by truck or SUV. At least one may require a four-wheel drive with extreme off road capability, that being Santa María. Two missions cannot be reached by automobile and require hiking or riding on horseback. Those two are San Pedro Mártir and Los Dolores Apaté.

The following list will be oriented as if traveling from north to south, the length of the Baja California peninsula. Included are mission sites as well as some visita ruins and water sources along El Camino Real. Map Datum WGS84

Baja California (Norte):

El Descanso 1830 ruins	N32° 12.33′, W116° 54.33′
El Descanso 1810 ruins	N32° 11.99′, W116° 54.51′
San Miguel	N32° 05.65′, W116° 51.26′
Guadalupe (del Norte)	N32° 05.52′, W116° 34.45′
Santa Catarina	N31° 39.63′, W115° 49.26′
Santo Tomás 1791 site	N31° 34.18′, W116° 28.83′
Santo Tomás 1794 site	N31° 34.40′, W116° 27.98′
Santo Tomás 1799 site	N31° 33.49′, W116° 24.82′
San Vicente:	N31° 19.80′, W116° 15.54′
San Pedro Mártir	N30° 47.41′, W115° 28.36′

Santo Domingo	N30° 46.25', W115° 56.22'
Visita San Isidoro	N30° 45.92', W115° 32.83'
El Rosario 1774 site	N30° 04.01', W115° 43.14'
El Rosario 1802 site	N30° 02.48', W115° 44.34'
Visita San Juan de Dios	N30° 10.95', W115° 10.08'
San Fernando	N29° 58.28', W115° 14.20'
Santa María	N29° 43.90', W114° 32.83'
Calamajué	N29° 25.26', W114° 11.71'
Tinaja de Yubay	N29° 10.69', W113° 59.26'
San Borja	N28° 44.67', W113° 45.23'
Santa Gertrudis	N28° 03.05', W113° 05.11'

Baja California Sur:

Visita San Pablo	N27° 42.13', W113° 08.70'
San Ignacio	N27° 17.02', W112° 53.90'
Visita Magdalena (pila)	N27° 03.49', W112° 10.18'
Guadalupe	N26° 55.16', W112° 24.34'
Mulegé	N26° 53.11', W111° 59.16'
Comondú Viejo	N26° 16.50', W111° 43.12'
San Bruno (fort)	N26° 13.95', W111° 23.90'
Visita San Juan Londó	N26° 13.51', W111° 28.41'
La Purísima	N26° 11.43', W112° 04.37'
San José de Comondú	N26° 03.59', W111° 49.35'
Loreto	N26° 00.62', W111° 20.61'
San Javier	N25° 51.65', W111° 32.62'
Ligüí	N25° 44.35', W111° 15.88'
Visita La Presentación	N25° 43.75', W111° 32.64'
Los Dolores Apaté	N25° 03.33', W110° 53.06'

San Luis Gonzaga	N24° 54.49′, W111° 17.45′
La Pasión (Los Dolores Chillá)	N24° 53.27′, W111° 01.86′
La Paz (plaque)	N24° 09.60′, W110° 18.99′
El Novillo	N23° 55.76′, W110° 13.52′
Visita Ángel de la Guarda	N23° 53.46′, W110° 10.25′
Santiago	N23° 28.54′, W109° 43.04′
Santa Rosa/Todos Santos-1	N23° 27.62′, W110° 13.15′
Todos Santos –2	N23° 26.98′, W110° 13.53′
Visita San Jacinto	N23° 14.57′, W110° 04.62′
San José del Cabo	N23° 03.73′, W109° 41.74′

Ruins at San Isidoro, once a visita of Mission San Pedro Mártir.
Photo by Tom Wimberly in 2016.

References

Aschmann, Homer. 1959. *The Central Desert of Baja California: Demography and Ecology.* University of California Press.

Baegert, Johann Jakob, S.J. 1952. *Observations in Lower California.* University of California Press.

Barco, Miguel del, S.J. 1981. *Ethnology and Linguistics of Baja California.* Dawson's Book Shop.

Beebe, Rose Marie and Senkewicz, Robert M. 2001. *Lands of Promise and Despair, Chronicles of Early California, 1535-1846.* Heyday Books.

Burckhalter, David. 2013, *Baja California Missions, In the Footsteps of the Padres.* University of Arizona Press.

Burrus, Ernest J., S.J. 1967. *Wenceslaus Linck's Diary of his 1766 Expedition to Northern Baja California.* Dawson's Book Shop.

------. 1971. *Juan María de Salvatierra, S.J., Selected Letters about Lower California.* Dawson's Book Shop.

------. 1984. *Jesuit Relations, Baja California, 1716-1762.* Dawson's Book Shop.

Clavigero, Don Francisco Javier, S.J. 1937. *The History of [Lower] California.* Stanford University Press.

Crosby, Harry. 1994. *Antigua California, Mission and Colony on the Peninsular Frontier, 1697-1768.* University of New Mexico Press.

------. 1974. *The King's Highway in Baja California, An Adventure into the History and Lore of a Forgotten Region.* Copley Books.

Dunne, Peter Masten, S.J. 1968. *Black Robes in Lower California.* University of California Press.

Engelhardt, Zephyrin, O.F.M. 1929. *The Missions and Missionaries of California, Volume 1, Lower California.* Mission Santa Barbara.

Gerhard, Peter and Gulick, Howard. 1956. *Lower California Guidebook.* Arthur H. Clark Company.

Hittell, Theodore H. 1880. *El Triunfo de la Cruz, The First Ship Built in the Californias.* California Historical Society.

Jackson, Robert H. 1994. *Indian Population Decline, The Missions of Northwestern New Spain, 1687-1840*. University of New Mexico Press.

------. 2005. *Missions and the Frontiers of Spanish America*. Pentacle Press.

Kurillo, Max and Kier, David. 2013. *The Old Missions of Baja & Alta California, 1697-1834*. M & E Books.

Martínez, Pablo L. 1960. *A History of Lower California*. Editorial Baja California.

Mathes, Dr. W. Michael. 1977. *The Mission of Baja California, 1683-1849, An Historical-Photographic Survey*. Editorial Aristos.

------. 2009. *The Land of Calafia: A Brief History of Peninsular California, (1533-1848)*. Corredor Histórico Carem.

Meigs, Peveril. 1935. *The Dominican Mission Frontier of Lower California*. University of California Press.

Nápoli, Ignacio María, S.J. 1970. *The Cora Indians of Baja California, The Relacion of Father Ignacio Nápoli, S.J., September 20, 1721*. Dawson's Book Shop.

Nieser, Albert Bertrand, O.P. 1960. *The Dominican Mission Foundations in Baja California, 1769-1822*. Loyola University Dissertations.

North, Arthur Walbridge. 1910. *Camp and Camino in Lower California*. Baker & Taylor Company.

O'Neil, Ann and O'Neil, Don. 2001. *Loreto, Baja California, First Mission and Capital of Spanish California*. Tio Press.

Pepper, Choral. 1973. *Baja California: Vanished Missions, Lost Treasures, Strange Stories Tall and True.* Ward Ritchie Press.

Píccolo, Francisco María, S.J. 1967. *Informe on the New Province of California, 1702.* Dawson's Book Shop.

Robertson, Tomás. 1978. *Baja California and its Missions.* La Siesta Press.

Sáles, Luis, O.P. 1956. *Observations on California, 1772-1790.* Dawson's Book Shop.

Taraval, Sigismundo, S.J. 1931. *The Indian Uprising in Lower California, 1734-1737.* The Quivira Society.

Tiscareno, Froy and Robinson, John W. 1969. *José Joaquín Arrillaga Diary of His Surveys of the Frontier, 1796.* Dawson's Book Shop.

Vernon, Edward W. 2002. *Las Misiones Antiguas: The Spanish Missions of Baja California, 1683-1855.* Viejo Press.

------. 2009. *A Maritime History of Baja California.* Viejo Press.

Weber, Msgr. Francis J. 1968. *The Missions & Missionaries of Baja California.* Dawson's Book Shop.

------. 1979. *The Peninsular California Missions, 1808-1880.* Libra Press Limited.

Werschkul, Dave. 2003. *Saints and Demons in a Desert Wilderness.* Xlibris Corporation.

Wheelock, Walt. 1971. *Byroads of Baja.* La Siesta Press.

Zevallos, Francisco. 1968. *The Apostolic Life of Fernando Consag, Explorer of Lower California.* Dawson's Book Shop.

Index

221

About the Author

David Kier has traveled the peninsula of Baja California for over fifty years. The history and geology of this rugged land has been a source of fascination that inspired him to research its past history and document his travels in Baja California. In 2014, he made some brief appearances on the television show, *Trail of Missions* with Cameron Steele lecturing at two missions. The website http://vivabaja.com is where many of his trips and collected data can be viewed. David Kier is a member of the *California Mission Study Association* and the *California Missions Foundation*. In 2017-2018, David Kier traveled over 15,000 miles in Baja California researching for a new road guide and visited many of the mission locations.

Books by David Kier

1973. *Baja and the Transpeninsular Highway.* Self-Published.

1975. *Kier's Baja Roadguide.* Baja California Bulletin, Special Edition.

1992. *Irrigation Design* (with Larry Hawes). Hydro-Tech Publications.

2012. *The Old Missions of Baja & Alta California, 1697-1834* (with Max Kurillo). M & E Books.

Travel and History Articles by David Kier

http://www.bajabound.com/bajaadventures/bajatravel/
The Melchior Díaz story:
https://www.bajabound.com/bajaadventures/bajatravel/se
arching_for_melchior_diaz.php

News and Updates:

http://facebook.com/oldmissions and join our group page.

Questions, comments, discussion?

Please email the author: oldmissions@gmail.com

To order additional copies of this or other California and Baja California history books: http://oldmissions.com

BAJABOUND.com
MEXICAN INSURANCE SERVICES
Are you Baja Bound? Visit BajaBound.com for the easiest way to get Mexican auto insurance! Buy and print out your policy in minutes with our easy to use website!
www.bajabound.com